Toronto's LOCAL MOVIE THEATRES OF YESTERYEAR

Toronto's LOCAL MOVIE THEATRES OF YESTERYEAR

Brought Back to Thrill You Again!

DOUG TAYLOR

AUTHOR OF

Toronto Theatres

AND THE GOLDEN AGE OF THE SILVER SCREEN

DUNDURN
TORONTO

Editor: Cheryl Hawley
Design: Jennifer Gallinger
Cover design: Courtney Horner
Cover image: ©Rosmarie Voegtli
Printer: Webcom
Except where indicated, all modern photos were taken by the author.

Library and Archives Canada Cataloguing in Publication

Taylor, Doug, 1938-, author
    Toronto's local movie theatres of yesteryear : brought back to thrill you again / Doug Taylor.

Includes index.
Issued in print and electronic formats.
ISBN 978-1-4597-3342-8 (paperback).--ISBN 978-1-4597-3343-5 (pdf).--
ISBN 978-1-4597-3344-2 (epub)

    1. Motion picture theaters--Ontario--Toronto--History. I. Title.

PN1993.5.C3T39 2016   791.4309713'541   C2016-900232-2
                                              C2016-900233-0

1 2 3 4 5   20 19 18 17 16

Conseil des Arts du Canada   Canada Council for the Arts   Canada   ONTARIO ARTS COUNCIL CONSEIL DES ARTS DE L'ONTARIO an Ontario government agency un organisme du gouvernement de l'Ontario

We acknowledge the support of the Canada Council for the Arts and the Ontario Arts Council for our publishing program. We also acknowledge the financial support of the Government of Canada through the Canada Book Fund and Livres Canada Books, and the Government of Ontario through the Ontario Book Publishing Tax Credit and the Ontario Media Development Corporation.

Care has been taken to trace the ownership of copyright material used in this book. The author and the publisher welcome any information enabling them to rectify any references or credits in subsequent editions.

— J. Kirk Howard, President

The publisher is not responsible for websites or their content unless they are owned by the publisher.

Printed and bound in Canada.

VISIT US AT
Dundurn.com | @dundurnpress | Facebook.com/dundurnpress | Pinterest.com/dundurnpress

Dundurn
3 Church Street, Suite 500
Toronto, Ontario, Canada
M5E 1M2

CONTENTS

On *April 7, 1956,* the occasion of the demolition of Toronto's famous Victoria Theatre at Richmond and Victoria Street, Herbert Whittaker wrote in the *Globe and Mail,*

I thought of the Victoria at this moment being razed to make a parking lot. I wondered if someday, somebody else would be naming theatres which no longer existed …

A city is bound together by its happy hours, by the memories of exciting nights spent in mutual laughter or tears at a mimic show. How many happy hours of the past are made anchorless by the demolition of the Victoria?

… Let them tear down the Victoria. Let them put a parking lot there. What I stand for is glory and colour and communication, and laughter and tears, and thrilling voices sounding out and the roar of applause to follow. What will the parking lot leave behind it, when automobiles are obsolete and gasoline outmoded?

Much of my sexual, academic, and social education did not occur in school or within my home, but rather in the movie theatres of my youth. When I was a boy in the 1940s, and later as a teenager, they were the most important centres of entertainment in every neighbourhood throughout Toronto, their only rivals being the local churches, which held social events as well as services of worship.

Despite the popularity of theatres, when I was young the most famous entertainment venues in Toronto were Maple Leaf Gardens and Maple Leaf Stadium. However, I only knew about "The Gardens," Toronto's cathedral of hockey, from Foster Hewitt's radio broadcasts, and could only dream of attending a game at the city's baseball stadium, located at Bathurst and Front Streets near the lake. As a result, in my young mind movie theatres were "king," since they were relatively inexpensive and within walking distance of my home.

The Colony Theatre near Dufferin Street and Eglinton Avenue West and the Grant at Oakwood Avenue and Vaughan Road were our neighbourhood movie haunts. The Grant was not particularly glamorous when I first attended it, as it was almost fifteen years old by then. Its modestly sized auditorium was infused with the lingering hint of cigarette smoke and stale popcorn. In retrospect, I believe that its well-worn seats were held together with discarded chewing gum. The Colony was similarly of modest size, but it was newer and more up-to-date, although a movie palace it was not. However, the films I viewed within them taught me everything about life that a young boy needed to know.

I now realize that despite the shortcomings of my local theatres, when I became of age to attend them I felt as if I had attained sufficient maturity that I would soon be initiated into the secret activities of the older kids, who frequented the laneway behind our house after dark on summer evenings. My older brother had alluded to these rites of passage, though I was too young to understand what they entailed. I suppose the movies had not taught me quite everything.

Sadly, most of the theatres of my youth have been demolished. Even the great movie palaces that I attended as a teenager and young adult are gone, or, if they remain, no longer screen films. These include the Tivoli, Shea's Hippodrome, Loew's Uptown, University, and Odeon Carlton. Some of the buildings that were movie houses at one time have been recycled to accommodate other commercial enterprises, prime examples being the Runnymede, Allenby, Garden, Kum-C, Orpheum, Garden, Royal George, St. Clair, Paramount, Parkdale, and Brighton. Today, over the entrances of the buildings, a few of them even retain the old canopies that contained the marquees advertising the films that they screened.

Other theatres, such as the Elgin (Loew's Downtown), Ed Mirvish (Pantages, Imperial), Music Hall (Allen's Danforth), Allen's Bloor (Lee's Palace), and La Plaza (The Opera House), are presently venues for musical groups and live theatrical productions. Unfortunately, only the façades of the University and Loew's Uptown Theatres have survived into the modern era. The Eglinton and the Capitol Theatres are now special event venues, but at least they escaped demolition, the glorious detailing of their auditoriums restored to reflect some of their former glory.

However, some movie houses of yesteryear stubbornly live on and today remain active cinemas — the Revue, Fox, Regent, Mount Pleasant, Odeon Humber (now Humber Cinemas), Metro, Royal, and Kingsway belong in this category. They have not been lost, but I have included some of them in this book. They remind us of the golden age of the silver screen, when movies influenced clothing and shoe fashions, hair styles, cosmetics, music, literature, and commercial products like soap, shampoo, and perfumes, as well as expressions of speech. This remains partially true today, but not to the extent that it did in the past.

Some of the surviving old theatres are classified as "repertory cinemas," a term for movie houses that specialize in screening classic films of yesteryear, sometimes referred to as "golden oldies." The Fox Theatre at 2236 Queen Street East and the Revue at 400 Roncesvalles Avenue are excellent examples of repertory theatres. Others, such as the Kingsway Theatre at 3030 Bloor West, screen a mixture of older films alongside recently released movies. Humber Cinemas at 2442 Bloor West screens recently released movies.

In the 1950s and 1960s, the weekend entertainment sections of the *Toronto Star*, *Globe and Mail*, and *Toronto Telegram* contained three full pages of ads for movie theatres, with pictorial advertisements promoting the latest film releases from Hollywood and, to a lesser extent, Britain. People now Google the name of a theatre to discover the films being screened and their starting times, and the listings in the daily newspapers are confined to a single page; they contain no pictures and often do not indicate who is starring in the films.

In decades past, each year during the final weeks of November, many movies had their debut to coincide with the yuletide season and also special screenings for New Year's Eve. The film *Holiday Inn* was released in November 1942, and included Irving Berlin's Christmas classic "White Christmas." Bing Crosby had originally introduced the song on his radio program in 1941, but it was the film that truly made it famous. Similarly, the film *White Christmas* was released in November 1954 to attract holiday moviegoers.

This was also true at Easter time. Some films, though not originally having debuted near Easter, were often re-released in ensuing springs to capture the spirit of the Lenten season, as their stories were biblical. They became perennial favourites of Easter, and this tradition continues today on television. These films include *Easter Parade* (1948), *The Robe* (1953), *The Ten Commandments* (1956), and *Ben Hur* (1959).

The first film released in the wide-screen format known as Cinemascope was *The Robe*, starring Richard Burton, Jean Simmons, and Victor Mature. It also premiered at the University. Advertising for Cinemascope boasted, "You don't need glasses," referring to the cardboard glasses required to view 3-D film, a format that had preceded Cinemascope. This claim ended the appeal of 3-D films until it was revived several decades later.

As a child, I viewed the old movie theatres as places to escape the extremes of the Canadian climate. During the sultry days of summer, when I grew tired of visiting Crang's swimming pool near Oakwood and St. Clair Avenues or travelling down to the lake to dip in the chilly waters at Sunnyside Beach, I escaped to the air-conditioned comfort of a theatre. My friends and I attended a Saturday afternoon matinee with the same enthusiasm that we had for the last day of school in June.

Similarly, when we wanted a change from sledding and skating, we hid from winter's frigid temperatures in the cozy darkness of a local theatre to watch "swashbuckling" (there's a word you don't often hear anymore) pirates, cowboys, crime-fighters, superheroes, and soldiers of valour. As teenagers, even on a frosty winter's night, we ventured forth to enjoy the thrills of the silver screen. Attending the movies was high adventure, generating excitement that few other experiences in my young life were capable of offering.

The world of film was my form of escapism, long before I had ever heard of the term. It allowed me to visit exciting foreign lands and exotic climes. Science fiction films such as *The Day the Earth Stood Still* (1951), starring Michael Rennie, and *It Came from Outer Space* (1953), with Richard Carlson, introduced me to the adventures of outer space. For some people, films retain this role today — exploring the past, reflecting our present-day lives, and peering into the future.

In decades past, newspaper articles about Hollywood studios and movie stars were numerous. Every newsstand sold a wide assortment of magazines that catered to the public's desire for the latest gossip and scandals surrounding the movie stars. This remains partially true today, but not to the same extent, as there is more competition from other types of entertainment. Modern movie magazines and social media are also more graphic and approach subjects that in past decades were taboo.

During the 1940s and 1950s, movies captured my imagination more than professional sports. I was unfamiliar with the faces of hockey and baseball players until my family purchased our first TV set; however, I recognized many movie stars because I attended Saturday afternoon matinees every week at a local theatre. In 2-cent packages of bubble gum, along with the usual piece of pink gum, companies inserted collectable movie-star cards instead of hockey or baseball cards.

Today, despite the dominance of TV and other electronic formats for viewing films, a few of the old theatres have survived into the modern era, as mentioned. Some have been lovingly restored by owners who realize that many people still enjoy walking to a local movie house where they can view films on a wide screen with an excellent sound system.

The appeal of the large-screen format, as opposed to television, iPads, tablets, or other electronic devices, is evident at the Bell Lightbox, the home of the Toronto International Film Festival (TIFF). It regularly screens films from the golden age of Hollywood. Many of them are available on TV stations such as TCM, but viewing them on the big screen, with Dolby sound, is totally different. Watching a comedy in a theatre as part of a large audience creates hilarity that can rarely be experienced when a person is alone or in the company of only a few people. Similarly, dramatic scenes in movies are more suspenseful when shared with others.

When Hollywood commenced producing movies, studios did not foresee that in the future their films would be viewed on tiny screens. The large-screen format was essential for many of the action scenes and sweeping landscapes. In order to format movies for television, many of them were cropped, or as the industry prefers to say "letter-boxed." This means that a portion of the picture that the cameras originally filmed was blocked. This is one of the reasons why people are sometimes disappointed when they watch a film on TV, and say, "It was not as good as when I saw it in the theatre." On TV, not only are the big-screen format and the emotional impact of sharing a film with an audience missing, but for some films a portion of the picture has been deleted.

A few years ago I attended a concert at Roy Thomson Hall when the Toronto Symphony Orchestra was performing the music for a series of animated cartoons, as opposed to playing the recorded soundtracks. The cartoons were mostly old-time favourites — Bugs Bunny, Mighty Mouse, Daffy Duck, Sylvester the Cat, and Elmer Fudd. The music was from the classics — Beethoven, Wagner, Strauss. It was fascinating to listen to the orchestra synchronize its entries, rhythms, and crescendos to match the movements of the characters on the huge screen. I had never realized how often Porky Pig, Yosemite Sam, and other cartoon characters crept across the screen to perform their nefarious deeds to the accompaniment of the music of Edvard Grieg's "In the Hall of the Mountain King."

There were many children in the audience at Roy Thomson Hall, as might be expected, their reactions loud and enthusiastic. However, it was obvious that the delight created by the cartoons was shared by the adults as well. It was not the music alone that entranced them. It was viewing the pictures on the big screen, where the artistry and creativity of the cartooning was obvious to all. The pictures were seen in their entirety, not diminished by the small-screen format of TV. It was wonderful to enjoy the creations of the old masters of cartooning as they were intended to be viewed.

On that afternoon, as I watched the hand-drawn characters, I recalled the thrill I had experienced as a child when attending Saturday afternoon matinees. Similarly, when I see films from earlier decades on a screen at the Bell Lightbox, I am whisked away to the days of my youth. It is an insult to viewers to take a creative work and allow media companies to screen it in a reduced format, as has been done to films on TV and other electronic devices. We would never visit an art gallery that displayed their collections in any other size than the one the artist intended and would never tolerate a portion of the canvas being hidden. I admit that the modern formats are far more convenient for viewers, but the quality of the experience has been greatly reduced.

During TIFF 2014 I listened to an interview with a film director who claimed that the special effects in modern films are superior to those of the past. What else would he say? After all, his aim was to promote his most recent film. There is little doubt that the computerized images of today are bigger, louder, and more spectacular than the special effects of yesteryear. However, because the audience is aware that a stunt is computer generated, there is not as much emotional involvement. Those who create computerized effects seem to believe that bigger, louder, and more explosive are best. The overall effect loses its impact as the special effects are severely overdone and repeated too many times. Similarly, a gag that is hilarious the first time it is performed becomes a bore when it appears again and again in the same production.

Several months ago, I saw in a *TV Guide* that the 1938 film *Robin Hood* with Errol Flynn was on TCM. I had seen this film when I was a boy in the 1940s. The *TV Guide* stated that Errol Flynn performed his own stunts, so I decided to watch the film for a few minutes. I watched the entire film, as the stunt scenes were indeed amazing. Even though they were not as spectacular as in modern films, they were real. Despite this, I realized that on the TV screen the film had lost its impact. However, the quality of the Technicolor was wonderful.

Because I was originally introduced to the magic of cinema in the old movie theatres of Toronto, I believe that preserving the memories of them is worthwhile, so I set about writing this book. My task was not without difficulties.

When researching the old theatres, I discovered that some of the surviving information is contradictory. For example, when I read about the Colony Theatre, located on Eglinton Avenue West near Vaughan Road, I found three sources that stated the Saturday morning matinees, referred to as the "Odeon Movie Club," commenced in 1952. Months later, I found an actual program of the Colony's movie club that was dated 1949. Contradictions such as these are common when examining information on the old theatres.

In another instance, I came across a photo of Shea's Hippodrome on Bay Street, its caption stating that the photo was from *Construction Magazine*, dated 1914. However, the film on the marquee was released in 1944, so the caption was incorrect.

There were other problems. Some of the information I found did not correspond with my personal memories. In some instances my memory was at fault, a prospect that I did not welcome but was forced to accept. There was other information that I was certain was correct, and fortunately I discovered proof. This made me feel better.

However, there was some information that I was unable to prove or disprove. When I posted this information on my blog (tayloronhistory .com), readers sometimes contacted me to offer their opinions, make corrections, or provide stories about their own days of attending the old theatres. I am very grateful to those who took the time to contact me. I always welcome corrections and further information.

In this book, I have tried to verify the information that I discovered, but, as stated, it was not always possible. I accept the responsibility for any errors that have occurred. Similarly, I have tried to credit the correct sources for the photos and apologize for any errors. I would be grateful for information that would allow me to correct any mistakes and place the revised versions in future editions of the book.

I am very appreciative of the staff of the City of Toronto Archives for their expertise and assistance in locating resource material and photographs of the old theatres. The information and photos in the Ken Webster Collection and the files of Mandel Sprachman, which he generously donated to the archives, were particularly useful. The photo collections of the Toronto Reference Library and the Ontario Archives were also helpful. Web sites on the internet such as blogto.com and cinematreasures.org, as well as silenttoronto.com (by Eric Veillette), were excellent sources of reference. Without these contributors, this book would not have been possible.

I am also indebted to Barry Long of Oakville, Ontario, who assisted in proofing the manuscript, offered suggestions, and contributed stories from his own days of visiting the old theatres. He also suggested adding "brought back to thrill you again" to the title for the book. I am very grateful for his assistance.

INTRODUCTION

Many people retain special memories of the first time they witnessed stories from books spring to life through the magic of the silver screen. Today, this occurs mainly within homes, on television screens or other electronic formats, and thus few are able to recall the first time it happened. This was not true in past decades. A child's first visit to a local movie theatre was an event that few ever forgot because it was the first time they saw a movie.

I was only six years old when I was first entranced by images on film. There is another reason that I remember the event after all these years. Strange as it might seem, I felt that I was indulging in something "slightly sinful." Nothing is more appealing to a child than participating in an activity considered by adults to be naughty. The reason for this attitude towards films relates to the history of movie theatres.

During the early decades of the twentieth century, films were shown in theatres that featured vaudeville and burlesque. Because these shows were considered unsavoury by many churches, when "moving pictures" were added to the performances, attending them became associated with iniquitous behaviour. In an attempt to legitimize films, theatre owners referred to their productions as "photo plays." However, they were not successful in creating a positive image in the eyes of many. Condemnation of movie theatres and films by some churches continued until the mid-1940s.

When I was a boy, my family attended a church that frowned on attending theatres. My grandmother referred to them as "dens of iniquity." However, on one occasion, the minister of our church decided to challenge the prevailing attitude by suggesting that they screen a film in the basement of the church as a fundraiser. The money was to be applied to missionary endeavours. I remember my parents discussing the proposal and the criticism of the idea from some members of the congregation.

Fortunately, my parents did not view movies as sinful, and we attended. On the evening of the screening, the church basement was crowded. The film that the minister chose was *The Sullivans*, released in 1944. Later it was re-released as *The Fighting Sullivans*. It was the true story of five brothers who enlisted in the navy and were assigned to the light cruiser the USS *Juneau*, which was torpedoed on November 13, 1942. All five brothers perished when the ship sank in the Pacific Ocean.

Needless to say, the ending of the film was heartbreaking, and I remember the tears running down my young cheeks during the scene when the navy informed the boys' parents that all their sons had perished.

The film screening in the church basement was a great success. I suppose that even those who had been doubtful of the propriety of screening the movie reasoned that the pleasure of attending a dubious activity under the auspices of the church was preferable to living with the guilt of attending a sinful event. Regardless of what drew people to the fundraiser, foreign lands were blessed by the wicked "photo plays." Amen!

My grandmother had not attended the church screening. As mentioned, like many of her generation, she continued to view theatres as undesirable places, despite the films shown within them being referred to as "photo plays." She had raised seven sons and instilled this attitude in them. However, in the 1920s, when her sons were young men, they pushed aside their parental upbringing and attended the movies. For the sake of harmony within the home, they did not discuss them in front of her. On the other hand, they surreptitiously talked about them with my grandfather, who, corrupted by his sons, became a willing convert to the thrills of cinema.

INTRODUCTION

In 1937 my father and uncles convinced my grandmother to accompany them to a local theatre to see the film *Captains Courageous*, starring Spencer Tracy and Lionel Barrymore. Based on the 1897 novel by Rudyard Kipling, it is the story of the perils of fishing on the Grand Banks of Newfoundland. For many years, my grandfather had earned his living as a cook on a three-masted fishing schooner on the Grand Banks. Urged on by my grandfather, my grandmother reluctantly joined her sons and attended.

This happened before I was born, so I have only my father's account of the event. He said that she passed no comment on the film, so they were never certain if she enjoyed the experience. She lived to be ninety-six, but never again darkened the doorway of a movie theatre. After the family purchased a TV in 1953 to watch the coronation of Queen Elizabeth II, she watched many movies on the small screen and enjoyed them. Perhaps it was the idea of attending a theatre that bothered her, not the actual films.

My grandfather continued to attend the movies. Many evenings he slipped away from the house on Lauder Avenue and went to the Grant Theatre on Oakwood Avenue. My grandmother did not approve, but she did not make a fuss. However, on one occasion he told her that he was going to visit his brother and instead went to the Grant Theatre. When he arrived home late, she suspected where he had been. A troubled conversation ensued.

He explained, "I changed my mind at the last moment."

"Are you telling me the truth? If you fib to me, I'll have to go to heaven alone," she replied.

With a sly grin he said, "Are you certain that you'll go to heaven? Remember, I knew you when you were a teenage girl."

My grandfather's saucy remark ended the matter.

I was a young boy at the time and never forgot the commotion that conversation created. I never knew that "photo plays" could be so problematic.

On July 20, 1969, when Neil Armstrong landed on the moon in the Apollo 11, my grandfather watched the event on television. He later declared, "The moon landing is a fake. I've seen better moon landings at the Grant Theatre and have the good sense not to believe that they're real."

Damn those "photo plays." They are indeed problematic.

***

Throughout my boyhood years in the 1940s, on Saturday afternoons my brother and I paid our 10-cent admission, purchased a 5-cent box of popcorn, and rushed down the aisle to locate our seats. After we were seated, we hoped that no kid sitting behind us would smash a box of Mackintosh's Toffee on our skull to break it into bite-size pieces. Flying spitballs were another danger, but dodging them was a skill that we all learned early in life. Similarly, flying popcorn boxes were a cinch to avoid. At the Grant, we also knew better than to put our hands under the seats, where the world's largest collection of second-hand chewing gum was located, framed by the steel edges of the seat bottoms like masterpieces of art in a gallery.

Before the matinee commenced, to entertain us and ensure that rowdy behaviour was kept to a minimum, they flashed the words of well-known songs across the screen. I think the theatre management considered this a cheap form of vandalism insurance.

Above the words of the songs appeared a bouncing ball, and scratchy recordings played the appropriate melodies from loudspeakers, located on either side of the screen. The result was indeed enthusiastic, though the Toronto Mendelssohn Choir we were not. Favourites for the singalongs were: "There'll Always Be an England," "White Cliffs of Dover," "Don't Fence Me In," "Don't Sit Under the Apple Tree with Anyone Else but Me," "Pack Up Your Troubles in Your Old Kit Bag," "Bell-Bottom Trousers, Coat of Navy Blue," "I've Got Sixpence," and "You Are My Sunshine."

After the singing ended, the screen darkened and the curtains majestically closed. There was a pause before the curtains swept open once again, indicating that the first feature film of the afternoon was to begin. Loud whistles, shrieks, and screams thundered across the theatre. It was a miracle that the ceiling did not collapse on our innocent young heads. Well, not all of us were innocent — there were a few older boys in the back rows sitting with their girlfriends who I suspected had been slightly corrupted by watching too many "photo plays." Perhaps my grandmother had been correct after all.

The studio's logo would flash across the screen. Universal Studios' enormous globe appeared with the word "Universal" encircling it; MGM's roaring male lion was surrounded by a loop of film and the words *"Ars Gratia Artis"* ("Art for Art's Sake"); RKO had a huge antenna, resembling the Eiffel Tower, perched atop a curve of the globe, radiating signals; J. Arthur Rank's studios showed a well-muscled man striking a huge gong; Paramount Studios' mountaintop, similar to the Matterhorn in the Alps, was surrounded by a ring of stars with the words "Paramount Studios." Some of these logos are still familiar today.

The screaming and whistling would become deafening when the title of the first movie appeared, followed by the names of the film's stars. The Grant contained 672 seats, and during Saturday-afternoon matinees was crammed to capacity. The noise was ear-shattering. After the name of the director appeared, silence would descend upon the youthful mass. This miracle was perhaps greater than Moses parting the Red Sea.

As well as two full-length films, we saw a cartoon, several trailers (previews of the next week's films), a cartoon, and a serial, all for 10 cents. Serials, also referred to as "cliffhangers," were film-plays shown in four or five parts, sometimes as many as fifteen, the ending of the story not revealed until the final episode. Among my favourites were those that I knew from radio programs of the same name — *Batman, The Shadow, Green Hornet, Mandrake the Magician, Lone Ranger, Zorro,* and *Dick Tracy*. Other popular serials were *Captain America, King of the Royal Mounted,* and *Superman*.

During the 1940s, the studios' star system was at its peak, which meant that the major studios held a group of movie stars under contract. MGM was the largest studio and had over sixty big-name stars under exclusive contracts. The system flourished from the early 1920s until 1948, when the United States Supreme Court ruled against the practice and ordered the studios to divest themselves of the theatres they owned in order to end the distribution monopoly.

As a boy growing up in the 1940s, my favourite movies were westerns, comedies, and murder mysteries, although I also saw many MGM musicals and war films. Big-name Hollywood stars dominated the screens, but British wartime stars such as Gracie Fields and George Formby were also popular. The names of well-known stars on the marquee invariably guaranteed a box office success.

From the beginning of the 1930s until the end of the 1950s is generally considered the golden age of the silver screen. Personally, I would include the 1920s, even though the industry was in its infancy and it was an era of silent films. My father, who arrived in Toronto as a young man in 1921, often reminded me how popular the movie houses of the city were all throughout this decade.

As the 1960s progressed, local cinemas began to shut their doors because of the increasing popularity of television. As more people purchased TV sets, attendance at the theatres diminished further.

This book examines Toronto's local movie theatres, which John Sebert's book referred to as "Nabes." The great movie palaces (e.g., the Imperial, Loew's Downtown, Loew's Uptown, Shea's Hippodrome, etc.) have been omitted. However, I have taken the liberty of including two exceptions — the Odeon Carlton and the University Theatres. As a teenager, I attended these venues so frequently that I considered them to be local theatres. I hope that readers will forgive my rather dubious excuse for their inclusion.

Most of the theatres included are neighbourhood venues, some of them not well-known as they were attended mainly by those who lived within walking distance of them. The ones mentioned that were located in downtown Toronto provided alternatives to the larger theatres by offering more than one film — sometimes three or four.

Perhaps you attended some of the theatres mentioned or your local theatres are among those that are explored. It is hoped that this book will create a few fond memories of Toronto's local movie theatres of yesteryear. For those unfamiliar with the theatres, perhaps a little of the glamour of the golden years of film will be captured. If either of these occur, the memories of the old theatres will not disappear.

CHAPTER ONE

Theatres on Yonge Street

Yonge Street was not only Toronto's main thoroughfare, but the dividing line between east and west, separating the city into two distinct geographic entities. Even today, postal addresses and street names reflect this tradition. Major downtown east-west streets have the word "east" or "west" attached to them (e.g., Bloor Street West, Richmond Street East, etc.). In the 1940s and 1950s few families owned automobiles, so those who lived on the west side of Yonge Street rarely journeyed east of Yonge. Those who resided east of Yonge rarely went west of it. There was no need, as Yonge Street was the commercial heart of the city. To a lesser extent, this remains true today.

In past decades, this east-west division was a determining factor when choosing a theatre to attend. Even in the 1950s, when I was a teenager, though I could easily travel across the city by TTC, because I lived west of Yonge Street I did not attend theatres east of Yonge. Why bother? The great movie palaces and other major theatres were located on Yonge Street or within close proximity to it — Loew's Downtown (now named the Elgin), Pantages (now the Ed Mirvish), Loew's Uptown (now demolished), University, Odeon Carlton, and Tivoli. Being centrally located, these theatres were attended by patrons from both the eastern and western sections of the city.

There were a few other theatres on Yonge Street not located downtown, and though not considered "palaces" had generous seating capacity and well-appointed auditoriums. These too attracted people who lived east and west of Yonge Street — e.g., the Hollywood (Yonge and St. Clair), Odeon Hyland, and Odeon Fairlawn.

However, there were some theatres on Yonge, close to Queen Street, which people attended from other areas of the city, because if they were already downtown, these venues provided a cheaper alternative to the big movie houses. The Biltmore and the Rio were two theatres that fulfilled this role. The Downtown, near Yonge and Dundas, was another of these venues, although it was considerably larger than the Rio or Biltmore.

The theatres located on Yonge Street that are explored in this chapter, although they were local theatres, were also attended by patrons from other parts of the city, since they were centrally located and on the city's main streetcar line.

RIO THEATRE (BIG NICKEL)

I remember the Rio Theatre in the 1980s, when it had seen better days and was surviving by screening three or four films for a single admission price. Because it was located on a section of Yonge Street that had become rather seedy, particularly during the 1970s, the theatre attracted people who were seeking a warm place to spend a winter day or to sleep off the previous night's inebriation.

However, the theatre had a long history and, in some respects, a noble past. The Rio was one of Toronto's earliest movie houses, opening in 1913 as the Big Nickel Theatre. In that decade, the admission price to attend a silent film was 5 cents — thus theatres were commonly referred to as "nickelodeons." Located at 370 Yonge Street, the Rio was on the east side of Yonge Street, a short distance south of Gerrard Street East.

In 1939 the theatre was renovated by architect Jay Isador English, who created a relatively unornamented façade with some detailing in the cornice. When it reopened, the owners changed the theatre's name to the National.

In 1945, Ben and Sam Ulster (father and son) rented the theatre. Ben Ulster's wife, Mildred, remembers when her husband managed the theatre.

Ontario Archives, RG 56-11-0-315-1

The Rio Theatre in 1946, after the renovations that were done in 1939.

He privately screened movies for friends on Sunday evenings, since it was illegal to open the theatre on Sundays. The movies were ones that he did not intend to screen publicly. The Ulster family finally purchased the theatre, renamed it the Rio, and screened first-run films. The front of the theatre was covered with colourful posters advertising the movies being shown and the coming attractions. Later, the Rio would often show films that were considered risqué, but it never screened pornography.

Unfortunately, the theatre slowly declined. A February 28, 1980, article in the *Toronto Sun* by David Kendall graphically described his impressions of the Rio Theatre during the years when it had declined. Mr. Kendall wrote that the theatre screened four movies, a new set of films offered twice weekly. When the projector failed and the screen went blank, patrons howled with displeasure and hammered the sticky floor with their boots.

When the movie returned to the screen, the roar dulled and it became quiet. It was then that you could hear the drip-drip-drip of the weeping ceiling. The leak was just to the left of the aisles, halfway down the theatre. It was caused by a broken heating coil in the ceiling. The area was cordoned with a rope to mark it out of bounds, as the manager feared that the section of the roof might fall down. However, patrons sat in the seats anyway. The movies (after the ceiling was fixed) were the same mixture of blood and breasts, but the young boozers, lonely immigrants, unemployed, and fantasy-seekers continued to watch with unaccustomed comfort. Mr. Kendall's description creates a vivid impression of the Rio Theatre in 1980.

The theatre was sold in 1991 and closed. However, the building remains on Yonge Street today. In 2016, an adult video and novelty store was on the site.

YORK THEATRE

Plans for the York Theatre were submitted to the city in 1914. Its architect was Charles James Reid, who in 1908 had been appointed the official architect of the Toronto Roman Catholic Separate School Board. Between the years 1910 and 1920 he designed many schools throughout the city. Reid also designed Shea's Victoria Theatre at Richmond and Victoria Streets, which had opened in 1910. It was usually referred to as simply the Victoria.

The York was located at 812 Yonge Street, a few doors north of Bloor Street. When it opened it was an exceptionally well-appointed theatre, containing almost 800 plush seats, covered with leatherette. There was a stage for vaudeville performances and an orchestra pit, but no balcony. A section at the rear of the auditorium was roped off, and the seats contained armrests. It is assumed that this area was reserved for smokers.

Unfortunately, the York was unable to compete with Loew's Uptown Theatre, which opened in 1920 a short distance south of Bloor Street. To survive, the York offered double-bill shows consisting of films that were not recent releases.

In 1937 the theatre was renovated and a balcony was added, containing 120 seats. In 1948 a refreshment bar was included, and in 1957 the

City of Toronto Archives, Series 1278, File 171

The view north on Yonge Street from the intersection at Bloor, c. 1945. The marquee of the York Theatre is visible in the distance, on the left-hand (west) side of Yonge. Unfortunately, this is the only picture showing the theatre that I was able to locate.

seats were all redone by the Canadian Seating Company. At one time the theatre was managed by the B&F chain.

My recollections of the theatre are from the 1950s, when it had become rather shabby. During the summer of 1955, I worked at the Imperial Bank at Bloor and Yonge Streets, not far from the York Theatre. This was prior to the bank's amalgamation with the Bank of Commerce to create the CIBC. My responsibility was to balance the bank's cash book each day. I must admit that I had a difficult time and spent many evenings working late trying to balance the ledgers. This was a decade without computers or calculators, although the bank did have a hand-cranked adding machine. I admit that this sounds like a description of work equipment from the medieval ages.

I also recall that the Pilot Tavern was not far from the York Theatre, as it was situated on the south side of the bank where I worked. The smell of the grease from the tavern's kitchen invariably wafted into the bank. The

Pilot was established in 1944, named to honour the Canadian pilots that served in the Second World War. The tavern became a hangout for artists and musicians in the late-1940s and early 1950s. It was later relocated to 22 Cumberland Street in Yorkville and remains there in 2016.

Because of my summer job, I still remember the York Theatre. The bank where I worked was demolished many years ago, along with the York. I was unable to find the year the theatre closed, but it was likely in the mid-1960s.

KENT THEATRE (QUEEN'S ROYAL, BEVERLEY)

I often passed the Kent Theatre when I attended the Hollywood or the Hyland Theatres, which were nearby. The Kent was located at 1488A Yonge Street, on the west side, a short distance north of St. Clair.

It was one of the earliest theatres that opened in the Deer Park area, which got its name because, when the Yonge streetcar line was extended north of Summerhill in the 1890s, deer were often sighted in the area.

Plans for the theatre were submitted to the city in November 1914, and it was to open as the Queen's Royal. This was most appropriate for the decade, as loyalty toward the royal family and Great Britain was strong. Also, in August of the same year that the plans for the theatre were submitted, the First World War commenced, adding to the patriotic fervour.

When the theatre opened, it contained 536 leatherette seats, two aisles, and no balcony, but boasted water-cooled air for comfort during Toronto's humid summers. The floor was of wood and tiles. The box office was located in the centre of the lobby.

In 1934 the theatre was renovated by Kaplan and Sprachman, and it is likely that was when its name was changed to the Beverley. The name Beverley was retained as late as 1942. There is very little information in the archives about this theatre when it was the Beverley, and I was unable to discover when its name was changed to the Kent. I was also unable to discover the year that the theatre closed.

Above: *View looking north on Yonge Street from St. Clair Avenue in the 1940s. The Kent is visible past the intersection.*

Left: *When this photo was taken on June 27, 1935, the theatre was named the Beverley.*

CAPITOL THEATRE

The Capitol Theatre was located at 2492 Yonge Street, on the northwest corner of Yonge and Castlefield Avenue, six blocks north of Eglinton. When it opened in 1918, it featured vaudeville and silent films. The theatre was commissioned by the McClelland family, who arrived in Canada from Kingston, Jamaica, and it continued to be owned by them until early 2015, when the site was sold to developers.

Mr. McClelland hired the architect J.M. Jeffrey to design his theatre. Above the marquee was a two-storey-high window topped by a Roman arch with a pair of Corinthian pilasters on either side. The cornice was unadorned, the overall façade of the building almost symmetrical. An article in the *Toronto Star* (February 2000) stated that the Capitol was originally named the York Eglinton, but its name was changed as there was already a York Theatre at Yonge and Bloor, which had opened in 1914.

Photo Ontario Archives, RG 56-11-0-274-1

Capitol Theatre in 1937. The featured film on the marquee was Wings of the Morning *starring Henry Fonda.*

Capable of seating 1,300 patrons, the Capitol was a considerable size for a venue that catered mainly to local residents, though it did attract some customers from other areas, since the Yonge streetcar line rumbled past it. There was a stage to accommodate vaudeville and a space near the stage for musicians. The theatre occupied the full three floors of the section of the building where it was located. The remainder of the building contained residential apartments on the second and third floors and shops on the ground floor.

In 1924 a balcony was added and more shops were included in the space on the first floor. In 1933 the theatre was converted to screen films exclusively. Further renovations were done in 1946 and 1947, but no candy bar (as children we referred to the confection bars in the lobby of the theatres as "candy bars," whereas Americans used the term to refer to chocolate bars) was added, to avoid competition with the Laura Secord shop to the south of the theatre's entrance. This was possibly in the terms

View from the rear of the main-floor level of the Capitol.

of the candy shop's lease. However, in 1954 a confection bar was finally added to the Capitol. One day in 1957 a fire in the stage area broke out late in the afternoon, but it was not serious and the theatre was back in operation the same evening.

The theatre remained independently owned but in later years was managed by Famous Players. In the late-1990s, it was a second-run movie house. Eventually the management was taken over by Festival Theatres, but they were unable to turn it into a profitable enterprise.

The Capitol shut its doors in November 1998, and for a few years it remained vacant. Eventually, after a two-million dollar renovation, it opened as an event venue, the Capitol Event Theatre. Though the seating was removed, the high ceiling, stage, and ornate interior detailing were maintained. A wall was removed to expose the projection room, which became a bar. There was a second bar in the balcony. In February 2015 the building was purchased by Madison Homes, a Toronto real estate development company, making the future of the property uncertain.

VICTORIA THEATRE (ASTOR, EMBASSY, SHOWCASE, FESTIVAL, NEW YORKER, PANASONIC)

As the nineteenth century progressed, the city's population expanded and development on Yonge Street spread northward. In the final decades of the century, homes and shops lined the street. In 1911, two private residences at 651 and 653 Yonge were converted into a theatre to screen silent movies, accompanied by a live piano player. The Victoria Theatre was born.

The mansard roofs of the houses, with their gabled windows, and the second-floor windows remained visible after the conversion. In the years ahead, the Victoria's name was changed to the Astor, although I have been unable to confirm the year.

In 1932, the theatre was converted to facilitate the showing of sound films and its name was changed to the Embassy. Some sources state that the theatre's name-change was in 1934, but Mildred Ulster, whose husband purchased the theatre, confirmed that it was in 1932.

Ontario Archives, RG 56-11-0-302

The Astor Theatre c. 1938.

In the following decades, the theatre's name changed several more times, becoming the Showcase and the Festival. In 1993, it was renovated and renamed the New Yorker. Between 2004 and 2005, the old theatre was mostly demolished, although the façade was maintained, and a new 20,000-square-foot theatre was built to host live theatre. The new building is eighty by fifty feet, with 428 seats on the main floor and another 276 in the mezzanine.

In 2008 it was purchased by David Mirvish and renamed the Panasonic. It presently features live theatre productions, similar to the "off-Broadway" theatres in New York.

I attended the theatre many times during past decades to view both films and live theatre. I always found it to be intimate and cozy.

HOLLYWOOD THEATRE

The Hollywood Theatre, which opened on October 27, 1930, was located at 1519 Yonge Street, on the east side, a short distance north of St. Clair Avenue West. The architect was Herbert George Duerr, who also designed the Major Rogers Road Theatre, located at Rogers Road and Rosethorn, and the Village Theatre on Spadina Road. The Hollywood's auditorium contained 1,321 seats, considered a mid-size Toronto theatre in its day.

The Hollywood was the first theatre in Toronto built explicitly for the "talkies." The first sound film screened there was *Love Among the Millionaires*, a romantic comedy directed by Frank Tuttle, starring Clara Bow. It premiered in New York on July 5, 1930, and debuted in Toronto the following October at the Hollywood. According to Mike Filey, Toronto's well-known historian, the film's soundtrack was played by a

City of Toronto Archives, Series 1278, File 8

Looking north on Yonge Street from a short distance north of St. Clair Avenue West in September 1946. The area on the right-hand side of the photo, where hoarding is located, is where the Odeon Hyland is under construction. The building to the right (south) of the Dominion store became the Flame Restaurant.

Western Electric sound system, which had been installed in the theatre when it was built.

The Hollywood was severely architecturally altered during the seven decades of its life. When it opened in 1930, on the second storey there were matching sets of windows on the north and south ends of the building. Each set of windows possessed three individual panes, the arches and pillars having Moorish influences. The marquee and large vertical sign above it were typical of the decade, impressive and of considerable size, but they did not hide the ornamentations on the façade. On the left-hand (north) side of the theatre was a vacant lot that provided parking for patrons. On the ground floor there were shops, located on opposite ends of the building. The box office was in a central position, the entrance doors on either side.

In 1946, the theatre was redesigned by its original architect, H.G. Duerr. By then a large shop had been built on the parking lot to the north

City of Toronto Archives, Series 1278, File 8, photo is by Ernest

The Hollywood Theatre, featuring the 1962 film Rome Adventure. *To the south of the Hollywood is the Odeon Hyland Theatre, where the 1962 film* Only Two Can Play *was showing.*

of the theatre. To expand the Hollywood, a second auditorium was constructed on the land behind the shop. The new auditorium possessed a north-south configuration.

The south auditorium, with approximately 800 seats, was employed during the day, and both north and south auditoriums were used in the evenings when there was more demand for seats. Eventually, to attract more patrons, a different film was screened in each auditorium. It is reputed to have been the first dual-auditorium theatre in Canada.

Despite the changes to the theatre and the much larger marquee that was added, the attractive façade remained visible. The Moorish influences in the detailing at the top of the façade had been retained, as well as the attractive second-storey windows. The shops on the ground level were removed and the space facing the street was employed for advertising the featured films.

In the 1960s, the theatre was renovated by Mandel Sprachman. The existing marquee was removed and the entire façade of the building altered. The windows on the second floor were covered over, creating a smooth, bland exterior. The price of the renovations was between $55,000 and $60,000. Throughout the 1960s, the theatre continued to attract crowds. During 1964–65 the film *Mary Poppins* settled in for a long run, and in 1970–71 *MASH* played for fifty-three weeks.

Despite the words from the song Julie Andrews sang in *Mary Poppins*, ("A spoonful of sugar helps the medicine go down"), the bitter medicine of the Hollywood's closure was not lessened in 1999 by an optimistic attitude. The wonderful theatre was demolished shortly after it closed.

CIRCLE THEATRE

The Circle Theatre at 2567 Yonge Street opened its doors in 1933, on the east side of the street, north of Sherwood, five blocks north of Eglinton Avenue. The architect was Eric Hounsom, who was employed by the architectural firm of H.S. Kaplan and Abraham Sprachman. In later years, Hounsom designed the interior of the University Theatre on Bloor Street West.

The Circle Theatre c. 1945.

Interior of the Circle Theatre.

Similar to most theatres designed by Kaplan and Sprachman, the Circle was in the Art Deco style, its façade containing strong vertical lines rising above the marquee. Contrasting with the vertical lines were bold horizontal lines. The cornice was relatively plain, divided into sections of varying heights.

The theatre's auditorium had 750 seats, but there was no balcony. The side walls were sleek and smooth, with horizontal lines, the corners near the stage curved. There were Art Deco designs on the rear wall and near the stage, with elongated light fixtures on the side walls.

As cars became more affordable and television became more popular, attendance at the Circle Theatre dwindled. It closed in 1956. The building was demolished, and today an apartment building occupies the site.

Many years after the Circle had been demolished, Bob Stevens, an usher who worked at the theatre for fourteen years, wrote a letter about his experiences, which is now in the files at the Toronto Archives. He wrote that when he started as an usher he was paid 50 cents an hour. When he was not guiding patrons to their seats, the manager insisted that he stand at a station that had rubber circular mats, which were very hard on the feet. After working his shift, he was very tired.

ODEON FAIRLAWN

Because the Odeon Fairlawn was located at 3320 Yonge Street, at Fairlawn Avenue, six blocks north of Lawrence Avenue, I considered it too far north for me to travel to view a movie. However, I remember the Odeon Fairlawn Theatre quite well. I thought that its appearance was impressive, with its sleek modern façade and enormous sign that towered above the marquee. Despite never attending the theatre, I was aware of its attractive lobby, as the spacious windows across the front of the theatre allowed me to view the interior. However, I was not aware that there was a small art gallery near the doors that gave access to the auditorium.

The theatre opened on August 14, 1947, built for Snowden Investors Ltd. They retained ownership of the theatre but leased it to Odeon

City of Toronto Archives, Globe and Mail Collection, Fonds 1266, It. 135137

Odeon Fairlawn Theatre in 1946, its marquee advertising the film The Best Years of Our Lives.

Cinemas. This was Odeon's first foray into the Toronto theatre scene. The company's aim was to present British films to a city dominated by American film distribution firms. Odeon Theatres was a subsidiary of the Rank Organization, which distributed J. Arthur Rank productions.

The theatre was designed by the well-known architect Jay English. Before working for Odeon Cinema, he had mainly renovated theatres — the Hillcrest (1930), the lobby of the Fox (1936), Centre (1940), Garden (1942), and Adelphi (Cum Bac) in 1943. Odeon was so impressed with the architect's design of the Fairlawn that in 1948 the company hired him to create two more theatres for the theatre chain — the Odeon Danforth (opened April 1948) and their flagship Toronto theatre, the Odeon Toronto (September 1948). The latter theatre's name was eventually changed to the Odeon Carlton. The final reference I was able to discover to the work of Jay English was that he designed the concession bar of the Radio City Theatre in 1951.

The Odeon Fairlawn Theatre contained almost 1,200 seats on the main floor and an additional 750 in the balcony. The film chosen for the opening was a British thriller by J. Arthur Rank productions, *Green for Danger*, starring Trevor Howard and Alastair Sim. In 1947, the film *The Man Within* played, with Michael Redgrave and Richard Attenborough.

The Odeon Fairlawn was a popular North Toronto theatre, where megahits that had sometimes premiered at other theatres were screened for longer periods. They invariably required advanced ticketing, which added to the prestige of attending a performance. A few of these films were *Lawrence of Arabia*, *The Blue Max*, and *Lord Jim*. *Funny Girl* played at the Fairlawn for sixty-eight weeks in 1968–70.

In the 1970s, the Fairlawn screened the same films as the Odeon Humber and Odeon Hyland, all three theatres offering them on the same dates. Also in this decade, the Fairlawn Theatre offered "Sensurround" films — the three movies screened were *Earthquake* (1974), *Midway* (1976), and *Rollercoaster* (1977). Sensurround was an audio system that added vibrations to allow audiences to feel that they were surrounded by the action they were viewing. Its effectiveness was questionable, as many claimed that they sensed nothing.

The Fairlawn was shuttered in 1985, its sudden demise surprising moviegoers. The building was demolished soon after and a nondescript structure erected on the site.

ODEON HYLAND

The Odeon Hyland was one of my favourite theatres. On Saturday evenings, I often travelled westward on the St. Clair streetcar to Yonge Street to view a film at this ultramodern theatre. Similar to those of the Odeon Fairlawn, the glass entrance doors gave access to an impressive lobby, fully visible from the street. Located at 1501 Yonge Street, it was midway between St. Clair Avenue West and Heath Street.

When the theatre opened on November 22, 1948, it possessed one of the largest auditoriums in the city, containing over 800 seats on the ground floor and almost 500 in the balcony. I remember that the

Odeon Hyland Theatre. The film on the marquee is Blanche Fury, *released February 1948.*

seats had dark-red-and-grey upholstery and that they were extremely comfortable.

In 1948, the film *Hamlet*, a J. Arthur Rank film, settled in at the Hyland. It had premiered at the Odeon Carlton but played for many months at the Hyland. The film was considered a risky financial venture as it was a film adaptation of Shakespeare's classical play. However, the directing and acting skills of Laurence Olivier prevailed and the film won four Academy Awards, including the best picture of the year. The film was seen by over 250,000 people at the Hyland, the Wednesday afternoon matinees mainly consisting of high-school groups. Evening performances were $1.50, but student matinees were only $1.00.

I remember seeing the film in 1956 in the auditorium of Runnymede Collegiate on Jane Street. Our English teacher had rented the movie to augment our study of the play. To this day, I am not certain that after seeing the film our appreciation of Shakespeare's work increased to any degree. However, in the duelling scene, Laurence Olivier's "skin-tight tights" created quite a sensation among the girls and inferiority complexes among the guys. I wonder if the reaction was similar in 1948 at the Odeon Hyland?

During the late-1940s and the 1950s, the theatre screened mostly British films, but during the following decades showed Hollywood movies as well. The films that I remember seeing at the Odeon Hyland are

Auditorium of Odeon Hyland.

Ontario Archives, RG 56-11-0-309

Tom Jones and *Room at the Top*. Both were considered controversial at the time and condemned by some of the churches. I am sure that this added to the popularity of the films. It reminds me of an old saying, "If a book is banned by the Vatican, the author will make a fortune." If this is true, I guess I'll remain a man of modest means.

The theatre was eventually purchased by Cineplex, but it was shuttered and finally demolished in 2003. Toronto lost one of its finest movie theatres.

BILTMORE THEATRE

In 1947, the architect S. Devore commenced the plans for the Biltmore. The theatre's owner was B.S. Okun, who leased it to Biltmore Theatres Limited. Located at 319 Yonge Street, on the east side of the street, a short distance north of Dundas Street, the theatre was only a few doors from the Brown Derby Tavern, one of Toronto's favourite drinking establishments. The tavern opened in 1949, a year after the Biltmore.

When the Biltmore opened in May 1948, the manager was Albert Perly. The theatre's auditorium contained over 600 upholstered seats, with a further 300 in the balcony, all of them installed by the Canadian Theatre Chair Company. Plush draperies stretched from floor to ceiling on either side of the screen, complementing the theatre's curtains. Though not luxurious, it was an attractive movie house.

In January 1950, the size of the foyer was reduced to allow standing room for thirty-five patrons behind the back row of the centre section. The same year, a candy bar was installed. During the building of the Yonge subway, the theatres on Yonge Street suffered, as the construction disrupted vehicle and pedestrian traffic. The Biltmore never fully recovered. After the subway opened in 1954, television added to the theatre's woes, further diminishing revenues; however, the Biltmore continued to survive as it was located in a populous area where there was a lot of foot traffic.

During its final years in the 1980s, the Biltmore featured five movies all for the price of $3, in competition with the Savoy and Rio Theatres, the three venues considered "grindhouse" cinemas. Martial arts and

City of Toronto Archives, Brigden Ltd. Photography, for TTC, Series 574, S 0574, id49412

Right: *The Biltmore Theatre marquee lit up.*

Below: *Auditorium of the Biltmore Theatre.*

Ontario Archives, RG 56-11-0- 271-1

action movies, as well as light porn, were the most frequently offered films. Many of them were classed as "restricted," but the rules were not strictly enforced.

Most of my memories of the Biltmore Theatre are during its later years, when it was long past its prime. The theatre had become dilapidated, attracting those who were seeking a warm place in winter to sleep off the previous night's activities. In Toronto's humid summer weather, the theatre's air conditioning had a similar purpose. It was an integral part of what became known as the infamous Yonge Street Strip. It was rumoured that in the back rows of the theatre people were performing sexual acts and other questionable activities.

John Farquharson, who worked as a projectionist at the Biltmore, informed me that the theatre closed in 1986. After it ceased to be an active theatre, it was often vacant or rented for other commercial events. It was eventually demolished and a modern retail store was erected on the site.

WILLOW THEATRE

The Willow Theatre opened on June 18, 1948, at 5269 Yonge Street, between Sheppard and Finch Avenues. It was too far north for me to have ever attended it. The Second World War had recently ended, and many houses were being constructed on north Yonge Street to accommodate the burgeoning needs of postwar Toronto. When the Willow Theatre was officially opened, the community viewed the event as a sign that Willowdale was no longer a backwater rural area to the north of the city.

Similar to most local theatres in Toronto, the Willow's Saturday afternoon matinees were the highlight of the week for children. Many of them spent hours in the cozy darkness of the Willow watching popular Hollywood stars of the era. As adults, some of these children related stories to their children and grandchildren about devising clever schemes to sneak into the theatre, or brag about how they successfully enticed a sweetheart to hold hands. As the years passed, these stories were gleefully exaggerated.

The Willow Theatre c. 1948.

Auditorium of the Willow Theatre.

I remember seeing the theatre occasionally, when I started driving. Passing it on the street, I admired the modernistic low-rise architecture and the immense height of the sign that rose magnificently above the structure like a community beacon. I seem to remember that it possessed vibrant yellow colours.

The theatre's architect was Herbert Duerr, and it was typical of suburban architecture of the decade. Large glass surfaces and glass bricks across the front of the theatre allowed daylight into the spacious lobby. The auditorium possessed almost a thousand seats, which the theatre advertised as "continental seating." There were forty inches between the rows, comparing favourably with modern seating arrangements, as Cineplex Odeon theatres today have thirty-five inches between rows.

The theatre survived longer than most local movie houses but was unable to compete for patrons when Cineplex Odeon opened a multiplex theatre near Yonge and Sheppard. The Willow closed in 1987.

DOWNTOWN THEATRE

The Downtown was one of my favourite theatres when I was a teenager. It offered double-bill screenings for a single admission price. My budget was tight back then, as I earned pocket money working weekends in a Dominion store. When my friends and I travelled downtown, the theatre attracted us as it often featured risqué films and horror movies. The Downtown was also located near budget restaurants and had easy access to the subway.

Sometimes we splurged and visited one of the better restaurants. On these occasions, one of our favourites was Bassel's, on the southeast corner of Yonge and Gerrard Streets. One of the few items on the menu that we were able to afford was a club-house sandwich and french fries. We felt that we had hit the "big time," as Bassel's was well known as a lunch spot for prosperous businessmen of the city.

The Downtown Theatre was built in 1948 by Twentieth-Century, at a cost of $750,000. Located at 285 Yonge Street, it was on the southeast corner of Yonge and Dundas Square. The short street known as Dundas

Right:
*Downtown
Theatre. On the
marquee are the
films* The Kid
from Cleveland
and Massacre
River, *both
released in
1949.*

Below:
*Auditorium of
the Downtown.*

City of Toronto Archives, Series 1278, File 63

Ontario Archives, RG 56-11-0-287-7

Square and the site of the theatre have now been absorbed into the modern open space called Dundas Square, opposite the Eaton Centre, on the east side of the street.

The theatre was a short distance north of the more famous Imperial Theatre (now named the Ed Mirvish). The exterior walls were yellow bricks, the height of the structure equal to four storeys. Including the ground-floor level of the auditorium and the balcony, it possessed over one thousand seats. The terrazzo-floor lobby was expansive, with a wide staircase leading to the balcony. Two movies that I remember viewing at the theatre are *Last of the Vikings* and *Devil's Angels*. Both films were popular and screened at the theatre for several weeks.

Because of its excellent location, the site was too valuable to resist the onslaught of the developers. The theatre closed in 1972 and was demolished.

ISLAND THEATRE

The Island Theatre was not on Yonge Street but on Centre Island. However, I have taken the liberty of including it among the theatres on Yonge Street as it was at the foot of Yonge. And besides, it does not fit into any other geographic category.

The theatre's location was unique as it was on an island in Toronto Harbour. The islands had been popular since the 1790s, when the town of York was established. Even in the eighteenth century, their idyllic mood and tranquil lagoons rarely failed to enchant those who visited their sandy shores or strolled under the ancient willows. In the early nineteenth century, a time when travelling to the hinterland of Toronto was difficult due to a lack of roads, the islands were a favourite place to hunt or picnic. This attitude remained until the final decades of the nineteenth century, even after hunting on the islands was no longer possible.

From the 1890s until the late 1950s, the islands were popular for summer homes and day trips from the mainland. However, in the years following the Second World War, owning an automobile became more affordable and those with cars began driving to the lakes north of the city.

Photo by John Milne, from the City of Toronto Archives, Series 1278, File 90

The Island Theatre at Centre Island, Toronto Islands.

The Island Theatre opened in 1951. The fifties were the last years before automobiles started dominating the holiday plans of Torontonians. Because of the popularity of the movies, it was deemed a profitable venture. The theatre was at 4 Iroquois Avenue, a short distance from the main drag, Manitou Road. Its concrete foundations were poured in March 1950, and the structure was completed by the end of the year. The Island opened its doors under the management of Charles Murphy. It possessed 705 seats, which included the balcony, where there were only three rows of seats. Access to the balcony was from stairs on either side of the foyer. The interior of the theatre was devoid of any artwork or ornamental designs.

Today, it might seem strange to open a movie theatre on the islands, considering that Toronto's summers are short and the weather is notoriously unpredictable. However, in 1951, in addition to the influx of summer tourists, the islands had a considerable number of permanent residents. Its school had 450 pupils and enrolment was rapidly expanding.

The first year the theatre was in operation, it was successful. However, in 1952, Torontonians suffered through one of the wettest summers on record.

Day after day, the rains continued, causing the water levels of Lake Ontario to rise. The islands were badly flooded. Manitou Street, the main street of the village on Centre Island, became a canal. Businesses suffered greatly. The Island Theatre was no exception. During the wet summer of 1952, the manager hired Durnan's Water Taxi Service to ferry patrons to the theatre.

The following year, attendance at the Island school doubled and the outlook for the Island Theatre seemed brighter. However, the theatre's attendance did not continue to grow, and its finances were soon in trouble. I sometimes wonder if the reason was because many people who travelled to the islands simply preferred the outdoor space, rather than sitting inside a movie house. I visited the islands many times during the 1950s and never once attended the theatre. As a matter of fact, I do not recall ever having seen it.

The final nail in the coffin was when Metro Toronto unveiled a new plan for Centre Island that did not include maintaining a residential community. Although demolition of the homes did not commence until the 1960s, the writing was on the wall.

Ontario Archives, RG 56-11-0-296-3

Auditorium of the Island Theatre.

In June 1956, a letter was sent from the Island Theatre's offices on the mainland at 72 Carlton Street. It was delivered to the Motion Picture Censorship and Theatre Inspection Branch on Millwood Road, requesting cancellation of the theatre's licence. Although the letter stated that they might seek to renew the licence at a later date, there were no further plans. The Island Theatre disappeared into history.

SAVOY THEATRE (CORONET)

As a teenager in the 1950s, I sometimes journeyed downtown to attend the Savoy Theatre at 399 Yonge Street. On one occasion, on a hot summer's day, I went by myself to a matinee. Some of the patrons appeared unusually rough, causing me to wonder if there had been a prison break at the Don Jail and following the escape they had all gathered at the Savoy. Being about sixteen years old at the time, I had a wild imagination. When one of the jailbird types sat next to me, I departed the theatre. Until I was older, I did not attend the theatre again on my own.

Many teenagers were attracted to the Savoy Theatre in the 1950s, since it was on a particularly active and quirky section of the Yonge Street strip. It screened horror flicks and restricted films, and did not vigorously enforce the age-restriction laws.

The Savoy was on the northeast corner of Gerrard and Yonge Streets. On the southeast corner was the previously mentioned Bassel's Restaurant, an eatery that occupied the equivalent of four average-size shops. After viewing a film, my friends and I thought that the restaurant was a great spot for a coffee and a western sandwich. Besides, Bassel's large windows facing Yonge were wonderful for overlooking the antics on the street.

Another favourite eating place in that decade was on the opposite (west) side of Yonge, a little further north of the Savoy — the Chicken Palace. In this restaurant they served deep-fried chicken, coleslaw, and french fries in a wicker basket, long before we had ever heard of KFC. In my late teens, when I attended the Savoy, one of these restaurants was often included in the visit.

Savoy Theatre c. 1963. On the marquee is the film The Three Godfathers, *released in 1948.*

Bassel's Restaurant at the southeast corner of Gerrard and Yonge Streets, on March 12, 1952.

The Savoy Theatre opened in 1951, a part of the Biltmore Chain, which also had theatres in the town of Weston (Weston Road and Lawrence Avenue West) and also in New Toronto (Lakeshore Road and 3rd Street). The Savoy on Yonge Street possessed approximately one thousand seats, including the balcony. Its yellow-brick façade was unadorned, its height the equivalent of three storeys. On the top floor there were small windows facing Yonge Street, the space behind them likely occupied by offices and perhaps storage rooms. The theatre's expansive marquee spanned the entire front of the building. The box office was situated near the edge of the sidewalk, to the left of the large glass doors that gave access to the theatre. At the front of the building, on either side of the entrance, billboard space advertised the current films as well as future attractions.

By the late 1950s and early 1960s, the theatre was slowly deteriorating. British Odeon Theatres leased the theatre from the smaller Biltmore chain in 1963, extensively renovated it, and reopened it as the Coronet Theatre. However, despite the upgrades, the theatre continued to lose business. The Odeon chain relinquished control of the theatre in 1978. It then became a true grindhouse cinema, offering as many as five films for the single admission price of $3.50. For a few years, it screened soft-core porn films. During this period, because attendance had diminished, the balcony was closed.

The Coronet was equipped to screen 3-D films, one of the most memorable being *Andy Warhol's Frankenstein*, a French-Italian horror film produced by Andy Warhol in 1973. Around 1980 the theatre featured a 3-D festival. However, competition among the grindhouse theatres was fierce on the Yonge Street strip, and as the theatre deteriorated, attendance continued to dwindle.

The building was sold in 1983 for over one million dollars and converted into the Jewellery Exchange. Its yellow-brick façade was covered with a layer of cement, which was divided into sections to create the appearance of large stone blocks. The building survives today, a reminder of one of the well-known theatres that once lined Yonge Street.

CHAPTER TWO

Theatres East of Yonge Street, on Danforth Avenue

Just as Yonge Street divides Toronto into east and west, Bloor Street is another geographic demarcation. On the east side of the Don Valley, Bloor Street becomes Danforth Avenue, often referred to as The Danforth, though in reality it is a continuation of Bloor Street East.

In the early decades of the twentieth century, the downtown core of the city centred on Queen and Yonge Streets. The downtown was viewed as extending as far north as Bloor Street. Loew's Uptown Theatre was not located uptown, but was given its name to distinguish it from the other Loew's movie palace — Loew's Yonge Street Theatre — which was downtown. As a teenager, I knew this theatre as Loew's Downtown.

Midtown Toronto centred on St. Clair Avenue and extended as far north as approximately Mount Pleasant Cemetery. North of the cemetery was considered uptown, its main arterial road being Eglinton Avenue. Uptown extended north of Eglinton for several blocks, and then the streets were in North Toronto.

Today, the boundaries between the various areas have changed. Because there is a great demand for homes and condos in the downtown, developers and real estate agents consider the terms downtown, midtown, and uptown to have more elasticity than an elephant's girdle. Anything within proximity of Eglinton Avenue is advertised as downtown, since this nomenclature increases the agents' possibilities of selling the homes or condos. In fairness, I suppose there is an element of truth to their deceit, as Toronto has expanded greatly during the last few decades and anything below Lawrence Avenue (Hoggs Hollow) does indeed seem like downtown.

At the turn of the twentieth century, the Don River Valley was an impediment to developing the land to the east of it. Bridges across the river were on Gerrard Street East in the south and at Winchester Street in the north. North of the Winchester Street Bridge, on the east side of the valley, it was mostly dirt roads, farmland, and market gardens.

However, all this changed in 1918 when the Prince Edward Viaduct (also known as the Bloor Viaduct) was completed. This is the same bridge that today facilitates the Bloor/Danforth subway line.

Development followed in the wake of the viaduct's construction. Residential communities increased in size and number, with Danforth Avenue being the main arterial roadway north of Gerrard Street.

It was not long before theatre entrepreneurs realized the possibilities of the area, since the communities along the Danforth required movie theatres within walking distance of the homes. Journeying downtown to attend a theatre was not convenient.

Soon, there was a string of theatres lining Danforth Avenue. When they were first built, they offered recently released movies. In later years, those that were of a sufficient size attracted patrons from nearby communities as well as those on the west side of the Don Valley. In this sense, they were not truly local theatres. However, in the years ahead, they survived by screening double-bill programs consisting of B-grade films or older films.

To the best of my knowledge, I never attended any of the theatres on Danforth Avenue, as I considered them too far to the east. In my eyes, they were close to Halifax.

NEW ONAKA (IOLA, REGAL, ACE)

The Ace Theatre opened in April 1913 as the New Onoka Theatre, but its name was soon changed to the Iola. It was located at 605 Danforth Avenue, on the southeast corner at Gough Avenue. When it opened, it contained approximately six hundred leatherette seats, but no balcony. The theatre's façade was unadorned, with a plain symmetrical cornice.

In 1939, the theatre was renovated and the number of seats in the centre section of the auditorium was increased to seven hundred. In 1945, the theatre was again renovated and its name changed to the Regal. At this time, its owner was Nat Taylor of Twentieth-Century Theatres, who in the years ahead partnered with Garth Drabinsky to form Odeon Cineplex Corporation. Nat Taylor's mother occupied one of the apartments on the second floor, above the Regal Theatre.

City of Toronto Archives, Series 1278, File 89

The Ace Theatre c. 1948. The film on the marquee is The Heart of New York, *a film that was originally released in 1933 under the title* Hallelujah I'm a Bum.

In 1947, the theatre's name was changed again and it became the Ace. The alterations were designed by the architects Kaplan and Sprachman, and a candy bar was included in the plans. The sign installed above the marquee of the theatre was purchased from the Ace Theatre at 39 Queen Street West (the old Photodrome Theatre), relocated, and installed on the façade of the theatre at 605 Danforth Avenue.

I was unable to discover when the Ace on Danforth Avenue ceased screening films, but it was likely in the mid-1950s. After it closed, the theatre was converted for other business enterprises. The building was placed on the real estate market in December 1969, at the listed price of $197,000. At this time, the site was occupied by a financial institution. In the 1980s, it was the Greenview Fruit Market and later it became a Shoppers Drug Mart.

The building remains in 2016 but is unrecognizable as a former theatre.

ALLENBY (ROXY, APOLLO)

On a warm summer day in 2013, I travelled on the subway to view the site where the Allenby Theatre had been located. Having always resided in the west end of Toronto, I had rarely ventured any great distance to the east of Yonge Street.

After exiting the subway at the Greenwood Station, I walked west along the Danforth. I was intrigued and delighted with the streetscape, as the shops, cafés, and restaurants were interesting and inviting. Finally, I reached the theatre at 1219 Danforth Avenue, near Greenwood Avenue. Locating the old theatre became the highlight of my trip. I was amazed to discover that its façade and box office remained as attractive as when the old theatre had first opened.

The Allenby started its life in 1936, designed by Kaplan and Sprachman, the prolific architects who created about 75 percent of the theatres in Canada between 1921 and 1950. The Allenby was one of the finest of all the theatres they designed in the Art Deco style.

Its symmetrical yellow-brick façade has strong vertical lines, employing raised bricks to divide the façade into sections. In typical Art Deco

Ontario Archives, RG 56-11-0-268

The Allenby Theatre, photographed the year it opened.

style, the cornice has rounded shapes and corners, and the brick pilasters are capped with stone. A central column of stone rises from the canopy and extends upward to the cornice, creating the overall effect of simple elegance. The canopy over the entrance is large, but it does not obscure the façade or detract from the overall design. The entrance contains an attractive box office, and on either side of it are shops, which in their day were rented to offset the expenses of operating the theatre.

The auditorium of the Allenby contained 775 seats, with no balcony. In 1942, the theatre received permission to allow twenty-five patrons to stand behind the rear row of the centre section of seats. The air-conditioning consisted of water-washed air, typical of the era.

In the late-1930s, the theatre inaugurated a children's movie club — the Pop Eye Club (the name possessing a double meaning). For 10 cents, children saw two feature films, a newsreel, and two *Popeye the Sailor* cartoons. In the cartoons, Popeye attained magical strength after gulping a tin of spinach. The Pop Eye Club commenced at 1 p.m. each Saturday. At these matinees, children were able to purchase a soda pop and a big bag of candy for 5 cents. Surely this deal was enough to make any kid swallow the contents of a tin of spinach.

Lobby of the Allenby. The film on the poster is The Walking Dead, *released in 1936.*

Auditorium of the Allenby.

I located only one complaint against the theatre in the files at the Toronto Archives. In 1947, someone observed that the matrons on duty were not in uniform. This infraction of the rules was officially investigated.

The name of the Allenby was eventually changed to the Roxy. *The Rocky Horror Picture Show* was screened there before it moved to the Bloor Theatre. For a brief period after this film, the Roxy continued to enjoy considerable success. Unfortunately, as time progressed, it was unable to compete with the popularity of TV. For a few years it was named the Apollo and screened Greek films. But this too was ultimately unsuccessful.

After the theatre closed, the building was vacant for a few years and in danger of being demolished. However, it was declared a heritage site in 2007 and finally became the location of a Tim Hortons. Today, when customers enter the coffee shop, they pass under the magnificent canopy of the old Allenby and walk past the box office where, in former decades, eager patrons purchased theatre tickets.

ALLEN'S DANFORTH
(CENTURY, TITANIA, DANFORTH MUSIC HALL)

In the 1970s, I worked for two years near Danforth and Pape Avenues and passed Allen's Danforth many times while travelling on the old PCC (Presidents' Conference Cars) streetcars on the Bloor line. Prior to the construction of the Bloor-Danforth subway on February 26, 1966, the Bloor streetcars travelled from Jane Street in the west to Luttrell Avenue in the east. Today, the TTC has only a few remaining PCC streetcars, which are only placed in service as tourist attractions during the summer months. On the occasions when I saw the Allen's Danforth Theatre in the 1970s, it was named the Titania and was screening Greek films. By that time it had become somewhat shabby.

The theatre has a long history that dates back to the early days of the twentieth century. In 1919, one year after the opening of the Prince Edward Viaduct (Bloor Viaduct) across the Don Valley, two entrepreneurial brothers, Jule and Jay Allen, opened a theatre at 147 Danforth Avenue, not far from the eastern side of the viaduct. It was on the south

The Danforth Music Hall, formerly Allen's Danforth Theatre, in 2014.

Allen's Danforth Theatre c. 1939, when it was named the Century Theatre.

side of the street, near the corner of Danforth and Broadview. Though the Allen brothers were young, they were not new to the theatre business, having opened their first venue in Brantford, Ontario, in 1907.

The inaugural screening was the silent film *Through the Wrong Door*, starring Madge Kennedy and John Bowers. This fifty-minute silent film was accompanied by vaudeville acts with comedians and musicians. On the opening night, patrons were amazed by the luxurious interior of the 1,600-seat theatre. During the next few years, the theatre flourished, as the Allen brothers had negotiated exclusive rights to screen Paramount films.

However, the Allen brothers overextended themselves financially and, in 1923, Famous Players bought their theatre chain, including the Allen's Danforth. In 1929 Allen's was renovated, converted to sound films, and renamed the Century, which screened mostly B-grade and older films.

In 1934, the theatre became a part of the B&F chain, which owned theatres such as the Radio City and the Vaughan Theatres, both located near Bathurst Street and St. Clair Avenue West, which were two of my favourite

Ontario Archives, RB-56-11-0-284-4

Auditorium of the Allen's Danforth Theatre.

theatres when I was a teenager. I still remember the towering sign on the Vaughan Theatre, at its pinnacle the letters B&F flashing in the night sky.

In the 1970s, the Century Theatre again changed hands, was renamed the Titania, and began screening Greek films, reflecting the changing demographics of the neighbourhood. In 1978, the theatre was renamed the Danforth Music Hall and featured second-run films and live shows. However, the theatre continued to deteriorate and finally closed its doors in 2004.

Eventually the theatre was taken over by Ellipsis Leisure Retail, which spent eighteen months renovating the building. However, after a few years the company was evicted for non-payment of rent.

The Danforth Music Hall reopened in December 2011, with improved seating and a new sound system. It is today one of the best venues for live entertainment in the city.

GROVER THEATRE

The Grover Theatre opened its doors in the early 1920s; its name was derived from the local telephone exchange. Located at 2714 Danforth Avenue, it was on the north side of the street, west of Dawes Road. It was a two-storey structure, with apartments on the second floor containing large windows overlooking busy Danforth Avenue. When the Grover opened, it was the most easterly of the theatres on the Danforth.

The Grover's symmetrical, neoclassical façade was relatively unadorned, including the cornice (the trim at the top of the building). However, stone was inserted in a few places to create an impressive appearance. The detailing below the cornice contained a row of dentils, this architectural adornment resembling a row of teeth. The term was derived from the Latin word "dens," meaning tooth.

Shops were located on either side of the theatre's entrance. They were an integral part of the building, providing extra income for the theatre's owner.

Despite the Grover's modest size, the sign above the marquee was disproportionately large, visible for a considerable distance at night, when the towering structure pierced the night sky.

City of Toronto Archives, Series 1278, File 81

City of Toronto Archives, Mandel Sprachman Collection, Series 1278, File 81

Above: *The Grover Theatre in the 1920s, gazing east along Danforth Avenue.*

Left: *The Grover Theatre c. 1939. Its marquee had been altered from when the theatre opened in the 1920s, and the sign above the marquee had also been replaced. This photo reveals that the theatre was giving free silverware to its patrons.*

The theatre became a part of the B&F chain in the 1930s. I did not discover much information about this theatre in the archives.

In May 1963, the Grover Theatre was for sale for $70,000. It remained unsold, and in 1965 was again listed at the reduced price of $52,000. In this year it was vacant, its canopy devoid of any movie titles. The theatre was finally purchased and became a place of worship for a church congregation. In the years ahead, the building was converted into a nightclub. It is difficult to determine how much of the original building remained after it was renovated for this purpose. Likely only the walls were retained.

PALACE THEATRE

The Palace Theatre was truly reflective of its name. It was another of the theatres that I passed many times on the old Bloor streetcars, often admiring its magnificent façade and impressive marquee. I always thought that it resembled the theatres near Queen and Yonge, in the heart of the city, rather than a suburban movie house. It opened on February 21, 1924, located at 664 Danforth Avenue, near the northeast corner of Danforth and Pape Avenues.

The interior of the Palace was indeed palatial. It contained almost 1,600 seats, on a sloped floor that started near the stage area, gently rising as it extended toward the rear. The auditorium's ceiling contained a huge dome, with a painted mural by a local artist depicting the meeting of Elsa and Lohengrin in Wagner's opera. The furnishings were silver-grey, and the seats were luxuriously plush, especially in the smoking loges. The lobby was richly ornamented with gold-coloured detailing, and on either side of the lobby were marble staircases that gave access to the washrooms on the second floor.

For almost eighty years, the theatre continued to screen films, but by the 1980s attendance had declined and the auditorium's size meant that it was difficult to fill. It became unprofitable and finally closed its doors in 1987.

Photo City of Toronto Archives, Series 1278, File 126

Palace Theatre in 1948, with a Jenny Lind Candy Shop on the west side of the entrance and Cameo Hosiery Shop on the east. Jenny Lind Candy Shops had green tiles decorating their interiors.

Ontario Archives, RG 56-11-0-310-5

Auditorium of the Palace.

PRINCE OF WALES

The Prince of Wales Theatre was typical of the local movie theatres that appeared on the main streets of neighbourhoods throughout Toronto in the 1920s and 1930s. It is not difficult to imagine children hastily skipping along the sidewalk, anxious to spend their pocket money to attend a matinee.

Located at 2094 Danforth Avenue, the Prince of Wales Theatre was on the north side of the street, near Woodbine Avenue, close to where the Woodbine subway station is located today. The theatre opened on May 5, 1924, six years after the Prince Edward Viaduct was completed.

Despite its narrow frontage, it extended a considerable distance back from the street. It was a relatively large auditorium as it contained 1,250 seats. Thousands of patrons entered the theatre over the years, but I doubt that many noticed the front of the building. Its attractive brick façade contained several narrow horizontal bands of stone, which gave the building a degree of individuality that separated it from the structures on either side of it. The theatre was topped with a heavy cornice

The Prince of Wales in 1927.

that contained a row of dentils (teeth-like ornamentations) beneath it. Above the cornice was a parapet that created the illusion of extra height. On the second storey were residential apartments.

There is very little information on this theatre in the archives, but it likely possessed a stage and an area to accommodate musicians, since it was built in an era when theatres featured vaudeville acts along with the silent films.

The film advertised on the marquee of the 1927 photo of the Prince of Wales is *An Affair of the Follies*, released in February 1927, directed by Millard Webb, starring Billie Dove. This movie is one of many from the era of silent films that has been lost. The fact that the film was being shown at the Prince of Wales the same year it was released indicates that at the time, the theatre was showing recent films in direct competition with the larger theatres on Danforth Avenue. The theatre shut its doors in 1966, but the building remains today, though it has been greatly altered.[*]

OXFORD THEATRE

Located at 1510–12 Danforth Avenue, the Oxford Theatre opened in 1928. It was another of the movie theatres that lined Toronto's busy east-west arterial road. Danforth Avenue was a magnet for movie houses due to the extensive residential areas located both north and south of it. The Oxford, located between Monarch Park and Coxwell Avenue, was one of the theatres that drew patrons from these communities.

It was an independent theatre, built by J.E. Wainwright. The building consisted of three storeys, with residential apartments on the second and third floors. When it was built, there were retail shops on either side of the entrance. I was unable to discover when these shops were removed.

The symmetrical brick façade contained no ornamentations, other than several rows of bricks inserted into the façade vertically to create a pattern. These were located between the second and third floors. The

---

[*] The author is grateful to cinematreasures.org for the information about the opening and closing dates of the Prince of Wales Theatre.

The Oxford Theatre c. 1937, shortly after it was renovated.

cornice was plain, with chimney-like projections at regular intervals. It possessed slightly more than 800 seats, on a concrete floor, the box office located to the right of the lobby. The air-conditioning was installed by Canadian Air Conditioning Company.

The Oxford was renovated in May 1937 by the well-known architects Kaplan and Sprachman. The marquee was altered and became rectangular in shape, with a clock positioned above it. An illuminated sign was also added to the roof of the theatre that advertised the name "Oxford."

In 1942, the theatre changed hands and was operated by B&F Theatres, before being shut down in 1955.

ODEON DANFORTH (REX)

The Odeon Danforth is another of the movie theatres on the Danforth that I remember well but never attended. However, I viewed it many times from the windows of the old Bloor PCC streetcars, which passed in front

View looking east along Danforth Avenue toward Pape Avenue on December 18, 1950. An eastbound PCC streetcar can be seen. The Odeon Danforth is visible on the south side of the street. The featured film was On Approval *(1944), and the movie completing the program was* Cavalcade, *released in 1933.*

of the theatre. The Odeon Danforth's main rival was the Palace Theatre, located a short distance to the east. Both theatres are now long gone.

The Odeon chain of theatres entered the Toronto market to screen British films, but later showed Hollywood films as well. In the 1950s and 1960s, Odeon developed the policy of featuring the same films simultaneously in several of its theatres. As I lived nearer to the Odeon Humber, there was no need for me to journey to the east end of the city to view the films playing at the Odeon Danforth.

On a hot day in July 2014, I travelled on the subway to visit the site where the theatre had once stood, at 635 Danforth Avenue. Today, a branch of GoodLife Fitness, a gym, is on the location. The site is on the south side of Danforth Avenue, a short distance west of Pape Avenue.

The Odeon Danforth opened on April 16, 1947, the only Odeon-owned theatre east of the Don Valley. It was impressive, its massive marquee dominating the street. The modern glass doors were recessed a distance from the sidewalk, creating an open space that formed a grand approach for patrons entering the theatre. This compensated for the theatre's small frontage on the Danforth. The box office was outside, to the right of the doors. Since the theatre extended back a good distance from the street, there was space for an extensive lobby, which was richly carpeted, with a wide staircase leading to the balcony.

The auditorium was large, possessing over 1,300 seats on the ground floor and balcony. The seating on the main floor contained two aisles — a centre section and further seating on either side of the aisles. Surrounding the screen were rich folds of drapery, which created elegance but also intimacy. The walls were decorated with sweeping decorative lines that accented its modernistic style.

When the demographics of the area changed, the theatre started showing Greek films and its name was changed to the Rex. Eventually the theatre was no longer profitable and it closed. Finally, the building was renovated for a fitness centre, but some of the interior architectural features of the theatre were maintained.

Today, whenever I pass the premises where the Odeon Danforth once stood, it is difficult for me to believe that there was once a grand theatre on the site.

CHAPTER THREE

Movie Theatres
on Gerrard Street East

Gerrard Street is another of the major east-west streets that had lots of vehicle and pedestrian traffic. The section of Gerrard Street west of Yonge Street is relatively short, as it stretches only from Yonge Street to University Avenue. However, Gerrard Street East begins at Yonge Street and extends eastward, passing through many local communities.

From Toronto's earliest days, the street attracted many commercial shops and businesses. It became the main street for people living north and south of it. Its potential as a location for movie houses was readily seen, with its first theatres being built in 1911.

BONITA THEATRE (ATHENIUM, WELLINGTON, GERRARD, SRI LAKSHMI, PROJECTION BOOTH)

The Bonita Theatre at 1035–37 1/2 Gerrard Street East was one of the earliest theatres that opened in Toronto. In 1911, two houses on the south side of Gerrard Street East, a short distance west of Jones Avenue, were converted into a theatre. The dormer windows on the third floor remained, and on the second and third floors there were likely residential apartments.

The box office was in a central position, the entrances to the theatre on either side of it. The brick façades of the old houses were covered with

Ontario Archives, RG 56-11-0-293

The Gerrard Theatre (Bonita) in the late 1940s. The featured films were Sweetheart of the Fleet, *released in 1942, and* Cloak and Dagger, *released in 1946.*

stucco. The marquee was relatively small, extending only a short distance over the sidewalk, although a larger canopy was constructed in the years ahead. I was unable to discover how many seats were in its auditorium when it first opened. It would likely have contained a small stage, as theatres in that era usually offered vaudeville alongside the silent movies. There was no balcony.

An entry on SilentToronto.com, written by Eric Veillette, describes an incident concerning the theatre that occurred in 1931. At the time the theatre was owned by Harry Lester, a prominent businessman in East Toronto. To increase attendance, he offered patrons free silverware. I was unable to discover what offence he had committed, but somehow the incentive resulted in police charges being laid and Lester being summoned to court. However, the judge dismissed the case. As a result of this judgment, giving free items at theatres for promotional purposes became common. It was not long before theatres began giving away dinnerware, autographed photos of movie stars, and even volumes of encyclopedias.

During the decades ahead, the name of the theatre changed several times. Later, it became the Wellington. In 1933 it was renamed the Gerrard. The theatre was renovated in 1947 and a candy bar was installed. In the early 1950s, the seating capacity of the theatre was reported as being 542 seats, and it was operated by the Allied Group. It was closed in 1965 and reopened in 1966 as the Athenium, which screened Greek films.

In March 1955, a theatre inspector discovered a young boy stretched out over two seats. The inspector chatted with the lad and discovered that he was eleven years old, and that he had been unchallenged when he purchased a ticket on his own. The boy claimed that he did this quite often. The theatre's owner was notified of the incident and was warned to enforce the age-restriction codes.

On November 3, 1959, a fire broke out in the theatre during a matinee with over 400 children in attendance. The fire was quickly extinguished, and after the smoke had cleared and the theatre doors opened to dispel the worst of the odour, the children returned and the matinee continued.

In 1957, it was noted that the theatre's matron was taking tickets at the door when she should have been on duty inside the auditorium. The inspector asserted that because the matron was not patrolling the aisles, the kids were noisy and unruly, and it was impossible to hear the sound track of the film. When the inspector reprimanded the matron, he discovered that she spoke no English. The theatre received an official notification about its disregard of the codes. In 1959, the theatre was again cited for improper supervision, as eight children were sitting in the aisle.

In 1960, the theatre's seating capacity was listed as 523. The following year, an inspector demanded that ticket sales at the theatre be halted, as several kids were sharing a single seat. The various reports of the inspectors illustrate how closely theatres were inspected in earlier decades. I wonder if this remains true today. We now live in a society that is more permissive about what is shown on the screen, but bureaucracy remains a formidable foe.

The Gerrard Theatre's auditorium.

In 1968, the building was for sale at the listed price of $54,000, but an additional $21,000 was sought for the business.

In the 1980s and 1990s it was called the Sri Lakshmi and screened films in Tamil. At various times the theatre was closed, but it always seemed to reopen. On July 12, 2011, the Bonita Theatre of old was revived and opened as an independent movie theatre, named the Projection Booth. It screens art films, as well as individually produced films and foreign movies. This was accomplished by the same people who reno-vated the Metro Theatre on Bloor Street West.

GREENWOOD (GUILD)

Originally named the Greenwood, the theatre was designed to be an intimate local venue with approximately 400 seats. The plans for it were submitted to the City of Toronto in December 1914, three months after the First World War began. The Greenwood was at 1275 Gerrard Street East, on the south side, a short distance west of Greenwood Avenue. It was a propitious time to open a moving picture theatre, since people were seeking distractions to relieve the stress from having loved ones transported overseas to fight in the trenches in Europe.

The theatre was successful and applied to the city in 1926 to enlarge the building and improve the premises, as well as create a new façade and marquee. It is possible that this is when the marquee shown in the 1937 photograph was built. The projection booth possessed a steel, fire-resistant floor, the latest in safety features. Though the seating capacity had been increased, there was still no balcony.

In December 1936, the Greenwood Theatre was again renovated, this time by Kaminker and Richmond. The alterations were completed in May 1937. It is likely that this is when the name was changed to the Guild. The seating capacity was increased again and all the seats in the theatre were changed to become self-raising, allowing patrons to enter and depart the aisles more easily. As well, two rooms at the front of the theatre were removed to increase the size of the foyer. A concrete floor

The Guild Theatre, formerly the Greenwood, in 1937.

was installed and the ticket office was encased in vitrolite (opaque glass). There was only one aisle, positioned in the centre of the auditorium.

The Guild Theatre (Greenwood) closed in 1951.

CROWN THEATRE

The Crown Theatre at 587–591 Gerrard Street East was located a short distance east of Broadview Avenue. H.P. Redway and R.S. Richardson submitted plans to the city of Toronto for its construction in July 1916. Similar to other theatres of this era, it was a vaudeville house that supplemented performances with silent films. The theatre was a small neighbourhood theatre containing fewer than 700 leatherette seats, its auditorium possessing two aisles but no balcony.

In 1936, the theatre was renovated by Kaplan and Sprachman, who preferred Art Deco designs, but there are only a few traces of this style in the 1956 photo, mainly around the box office. Therefore, it is likely

City of Toronto Archives, Series 1278, File 55

This poor-quality photograph of the Crown Theatre was the only picture available in the City of Toronto and Ontario archives. It was taken in August 1956, the year the theatre was demolished.

that the renovations of 1936 involved only this part of the theatre and the façade remained untouched. Perhaps the interior of the theatre was also renovated at the same time. The 1956 façade is symmetrical, with pilasters (faux columns) of brick that rise from above the canopy to the cornice, which is simple and unadorned.

One of the films on the marquee in the 1956 photo is *The Rains of Ranchipur*, starring Richard Burton and Lana Turner. I remember seeing this film at Shea's Hippodrome in 1955. A friend and I sat in the enormous balcony and thoroughly enjoyed the movie, especially its hot romantic scenes. Being teenagers, we thought they were quite steamy. I am certain that other teenagers had similar thoughts when they viewed the film at the Crown in 1956.

The Rains of Ranchipur was among the last movies screened at the Crown. The theatre was placed on the real estate market shortly after the film played, the asking price being $65,000. It was purchased and renovated to create a small shopping complex containing Asian stores and a market.

EASTWOOD THEATRE

Opened in 1927 at 1430 Gerrard Street East, the Eastwood was constructed in the Beaux-Arts style, with a symmetrical, relatively unadorned façade. Although it possessed a plain cornice, the trim below was slightly more elaborate. The faux arches on either end of the façade contained balcony railings. The three windows located behind the marquee complemented the faux arches, as they were topped with Roman arches. Beneath the cornice were rectangular inserts that resembled stone blocks, though they were likely composed of cement. Small decorative circles on either side of the faux arches were the only other ornamentations on the façade.

The auditorium, which contained almost 900 wooden seats with leather backs, included a small balcony and a stage to accommodate vaudeville and live theatre. There were box seats on both sides of the stage, an orchestra pit, and ornate chandeliers on the ceiling. Similar to most theatres in that decade, there were shops on either side of its entrance, which were rented to increase revenues.

Ontario Archives, RG 56-11-0-287-1

Eastwood Theatre in 1948.

Between the years 1944 and 1945, the theatre was managed by the B&F chain. In January 1946, an inspector ordered that a SOLD OUT sign be placed in the box-office window of the Eastwood. This was because its auditorium was filled to capacity, and the inspector had discovered twenty-one children seated on the edge of the orchestra pit. The manager explained that it had occurred when some children had visited the washroom and incoming patrons had occupied their seats. The manager insisted that there were no problems, as there were five ushers on duty, as well as a matron. The authorities did not take the matter any further.

The same year (1946), an inspector again visited the Eastwood and noticed another problem. Apparently, the only access to the projection room was via a circular ship's ladder staircase. He reported that when he ascended the stairs, the door to the projection room was locked, which was against fire codes. He also reported, "There was no drinking water available in the theatre, other than the water in the toilet boxes." The inspector's words seemed to imply that he considered the water in the toilet boxes a possible source of drinking water. I am certain that this is not what he meant.

In February 1945, a court summons was issued to the theatre's manager because he had allowed too many patrons to stand behind the back rows of the auditorium, where they blocked the aisles. Again, the theatre had ignored fire regulations, a serious offence. When a judge heard the case, the manager was fined $20, even though the maximum penalty was $200. The inspector who laid the charges was heard declaring that the penalty was too light. In 1961, another inspector reported that the theatre was in poor condition, attendance was low, and that many repairs were needed.

At one time, the Eastwood Theatre was managed by Bill Summerville, whose brother was Don Summerville, a mayor of Toronto. After theatre attendance declined, for a few years the theatre screened Italian films. Unfortunately, the theatre did not remain profitable and closed in 1966. However, the building was saved and converted into an East Indian centre.

Ontario Archives, RG 56-11-0-287-2

Auditorium of the Eastwood.

CHAPTER FOUR

Theatres on Queen Street East

Queen Street has been a main east–west arterial road since Toronto's earliest days, when the city was a small town named York, and Queen Street was known as Lot Street. In those years, the section of the street east of Yonge did not extend a great distance due to the swamps east of the town. The Don River was another barrier that blocked the town's eastward expansion. However, after the swamps were drained and bridges were constructed over the Don River, Queen Street was open to residential and commercial development.

As the nineteenth century progressed, pedestrian traffic on Queen Street increased as more shops and businesses opened along the avenue. People tended to shop locally, only travelling to the stores closer to Yonge Street when special household items were needed or for Christmas shopping. When "moving picture theatres" appeared in Toronto, it was logical to build them along Queen Street East so that people did not need to travel by streetcar to attend the theatres downtown.

REX THEATRE (JOY)

In the City of Toronto Archives, the floor plans of the Rex Theatre, at 1130 Queen Street East, are dated December 1914, the year the First World War commenced. The Rex was located on the northeast corner of

Bertmount and Queen Street East. It contained 381 seats, in an auditorium with only a central aisle, but there was no balcony. The lobby was a mere nineteen-feet wide. The box office was positioned on the right-hand side of the entrance, adjacent to the street.

The façade was plain with a simple unadorned cornice, although above the windows on the second floor there was a faux-cornice with large dentils, the only architectural detailing. A synchronous sound system was added to the theatre in 1931, which synchronized the sound with the visuals on the screen.

In February 1938 the manager and owner of the Rex Theatre's licence was Sidney Goldstone. In September 1941 air conditioning was installed. The following year, the owners hired Kaplan and Sprachman to renovate the theatre. The seating capacity was increased to 427 seats, which were covered with leatherette. It is likely that this was when the name of the theatre was changed to the Joy.

This modest local theatre closed in the mid-1950s.

City of Toronto Archives, Series 1278, File 10

Photo of the Joy Theatre taken c. 1946.

LA PLAZA THEATRE (ACROPOLIS, DUNDAS, CINEMA ELLIS, THE OPERA HOUSE)

Plans for the La Plaza Theatre were submitted to the City of Toronto in February 1915. Located at 735 Queen Street East, it was on the south side of the street, a short distance east of Broadview Avenue, near Lewis Street. The venue offered live theatre and silent movies, so they included a small stage and an orchestra circle. The auditorium of the La Plaza contained 560 seats, and in the balcony were a further 303. On either side of the stage there were two box seats, each with six chairs.

The three-storey, red-brick theatre contained residential apartments on the second and third floors and shops on either side of the entrance that faced Queen Street East. Patrons entered the theatre through a narrow foyer that led to a small inner lobby.

The La Plaza remained a highly popular theatre on the vaudeville circuit throughout the 1930s, but as the popularity of films increased, it became primarily a movie theatre. In October 1948, the rear row of seats was removed to install a candy bar.

Entrance and marquee of the La Plaza Theatre in 1946.

Ontario Archives, RG 56-11-0-278

View from the balcony of the La Plaza. This photo was likely taken in the 1950s, when the theatre was strictly a movie house. The box seats have been removed.

The La Plaza in 2015, now named The Opera House.

Over the years it changed names several times, becoming the Acropolis, the Dundas, and the Cinema Ellis.*

The theatre was for sale in 1963, and perhaps this was when it was purchased and became the Opera House. I have been unable to confirm this fact, but it was during the 1960s that its name was changed.

Today it still operates as a theatre for live concerts, with a capacity of over 800 patrons.

IMPERIAL (PALTON, RIALTO, EMPIRE)

The theatre that became the Empire was originally named the Imperial, though most of us who remember Toronto's old movie theatres associate the name "Imperial" with the magnificent theatre on Yonge Street that is now the Ed Mirvish.

The Imperial opened in 1915 in Toronto's east end and was located in the newly constructed Shepherd Refuge Building at 408 Queen Street East, on the north side, between Parliament and Sackville. Featuring vaudeville and silent "moving pictures," it had 762 wooden seats, but no balcony or air conditioning.

In 1922 its name was changed from the Imperial to the Palton, and in 1925 it was renamed the Rialto. In February 1936, an inspector's report stated that there was no urinal in the men's washroom, but only a toilet. The washroom was located at the bottom of the stairs, with only a flimsy wooden frame partition around it. The floor in the toilet area was wet and there was a bad smell. To make matters worse, the basement was often dark as teenage boys were constantly turning off the lights as a prank. Thus, descending the old wooden stairs was dangerous. The inspector insisted that the light switch be protected so it would be accessible only to employees.

In 1942, the theatre was renovated. In 1953, a candy bar was added to the theatre by removing seven seats in the back row of the auditorium. In other archival reports that year, the theatre's name was listed as the Empire. I was unable to discover the exact year that it became the Empire.

---

* The source for this information was theoperahousetoronto.com/history.

Salmon Collection in the Toronto Archives, Series 1278, File 88

The Imperial Theatre, later the Empire, in January 1919.

Photo from the *Toronto Telegram*, City of Toronto Archives, Series 1278, File 10

The Empire Theatre on October 11, 1956.

The author of the website Long Gone Movie Theatres from Toronto's East End (www.oocities.org/hollywood/club/7400/2003theatres.htm) wrote that the Empire Theatre was "… the worst dump I had ever seen … it was easy to sneak in but it was rumoured to be infected with rats and I had a morbid fear of rats, though I had never seen one." These remarks likely applied to the theatre towards the end of its days. The Empire closed in the early 1960s.

FAMILY THEATRE

Blueprints for the Family Theatre, located at 2173–75 Queen Street East, to the east of Lee Avenue, were submitted to the city in February–March 1919. It was to be built for W.F. Sexton. There was an existing building on the site, which was gutted and the theatre built inside the walls. It is assumed that the theatre opened in 1920.

I never attended this theatre or knew it existed until I commenced researching the old movie theatres of the city. I learned that it was a modest two-storey building, the theatre located on the ground floor, with residential apartments on the second storey, and, for a few years, a billiard room.

The Family Theatre.

City of Toronto Archives, Series 1278, File 70

There is an anecdote in the files of the Toronto Archives that tells of a projectionist who worked at the theatre in the 1920s. He often brought his young son to the theatre and seated the boy in the auditorium to watch the movies while he worked in the projection booth. When the man went home for dinner, he left the lad in the theatre. After the meal, he returned, completed his night's work, and retrieved his son. Apparently, the boy was delighted with the arrangement. It did not mention where the son received his evening meal.

The theatre contained a wooden floor with 546 seats purchased from the Globe Furniture Company. On either side of the entrance to the theatre, there were shops. In 1931, when the theatre was renovated by the architect Saxon H. Hunter, its owner remained W.F. Sexton. In 1935, the shops at the front of the theatre were removed to create space to relocate the washrooms from the basement to the ground floor and construct an office for the manager.

City of Toronto Archives, Series 1278, File 70

This undated photo was likely taken after the renovations in 1931, as the seating capacity has been increased to ten seats in the centre section. The faux windows with curtains on the side walls of the auditorium attempted to create the impression of a living room in a home.

In 1937, the Family Theatre was cited for having an untidy cellar. In the basement, where the furnace and the fuel room were located, strewn over the floor were cardboard signs, rags, and wrapping paper.

In December of 1948, the two rows of seats were removed from the rear of the auditorium to install a candy bar. However, sales at the new confectionery stand did not last long, as the theatre closed a few weeks later. It seems strange that it met its demise at a time when the movie business was thriving. I was unable to discover the reason.

TECK THEATRE

The Teck Theatre is a rarity in the history of Toronto movie houses, as its life as a theatre was one of the shortest on record. It opened in 1931, during the Great Depression. Perhaps the harsh economic times of the 1930s led to its early demise. However, most theatres survived the Depression because, despite people having very little money, attending movies was relatively cheap.

The Teck Theatre was owned by Jerry and Michael Shea, two brothers born in St. Catharines, Ontario, who later moved to Buffalo, New York. In Toronto, they built Shea's Victoria at Richmond and Victoria Streets in 1910 and Shea's Hippodrome on Bay Street in 1914, two of Toronto's great movie palaces of the early twentieth century. Thus, the Teck had investors of substance behind it. This makes its all the more surprising that it closed after such a short time.

The building that contained the Teck was unpretentious, its façade symmetrical, with few architectural details. The box office was in a central position, outside the small lobby. However, the canopy containing the marquee was impressively ornate. Its auditorium had faux windows on the east and west walls, as well as a simulated wall at the base of the stage, which created the impression that a person viewing the screen was peering over a low wall.

The theatre was located at 700 Queen Street East, a few doors west of Broadview Avenue, in the Riverdale District. The Riverdale Jewellery shop to the west paid rent to the owners of the theatre. The shop was

City of Toronto Archives, Fonds 1278, File 10

Teck Theatre in 1932. The film on the marquee is Delicious, *a George Gershwin romantic musical comedy.*

run by Karl Minoff until 1958. To the east of the theatre was the old Broadview Hotel, where the popular bar Jilly's was eventually located. Jilly's closed in 2014, when the hotel was redeveloped for other purposes.

The Teck was active as a theatre during the years when the industry was transitioning from silent movies to sound films ("talkies"). The Twitter account @tosilentfilm provides information about one of the piano players who performed the background music for silent films at the Teck. The children delighted in gathering around the piano when he played, listening intensely as his hands flew over the keys.

The theatre closed in 1933, after having been open for only two years. The site was renovated and used for other commercial purposes.

CHAPTER FIVE

Theatres on Other Streets
East of Yonge

Though many of the theatres east of Yonge Street were on major streets such as Danforth Avenue, Gerrard, and Queen East, there were other streets that were advantageous as theatre sites. They were also main arterial roadways, or were close to them, and thus the theatres were able to take advantage of the constant pedestrian traffic. Many of them were originally small local venues, but by the middle of the twentieth century some of them were a considerable size.

LA RETA THEATRE (PAPE)

The scarcity of photos of the La Reta Theatre is matched by the paucity of information on it in the archives. I must admit that until I commenced researching Toronto's old movie houses, the La Reta was unknown to me. It is likely unknown to most readers as well, as it was a small local theatre mainly attended only by those who lived within close proximity to it.

Because of the lack of information, I have examined the photos, along with the few facts that are available, and developed some theories about how the La Reta appeared when it was a functioning movie house.

It was a small neighbourhood theatre, located in East Toronto, at 336 Pape Avenue, a few doors south of Gerrard Street East. I was unable to discover the year that it opened, but it is shown in the background of a

City of Toronto Archives, Series 1278, File 110

This unattractive photo of the La Reta (Pape) Theatre was the only one available. It was taken after the theatre ceased to screen movies and became a bingo hall (c. 1958).

TTC photo that is dated 1928. Judging from its architectural style, it was likely built in the early 1920s or perhaps a few years earlier. Though the theatre was originally named the La Reta, it was renamed the Pape.

The building was basically a box shape, with a plain cornice and a small parapet above the unadorned front façade. There were residential apartments on the second floor. To the south of the theatre was a lane-way. The box office was close to the sidewalk, to the left (north) of the entrance. It's possible that there were originally a few architectural details on the west façade on Pape Street, which were obscured when the large marquee was added to the theatre. I am basing this assumption on the fact that its south façade, facing the laneway, has a few brick pilasters on the ground-floor level. Also, the canopy and marquee in the 1950s photo is not original to the theatre, as its style is similar to those of the 1930s and 1940s. The 1928 photo verifies this theory.

In the era when the La Reta opened, it would have shown silent films alongside vaudeville shows. To accommodate this format, it would have required a small stage and space for a piano, with a live piano player to provide music to accompany the silent films. In many theatres, the stages were later removed. Due to the height of the building and the fact that there were apartments on the second floor, I doubt that there was a balcony. The size of the theatre suggests that it likely had only a centre aisle, its seating capacity probably around 300.

Information posted on Long Gone Movie Theatres From Toronto's East End states that the theatre closed in 1955. It was vacant for a few years, but the Toronto Archives reveal that in 1958 all the seats in the Pape Theatre were removed to allow tables and chairs to be placed in the old theatre's auditorium. When these alterations were completed, it reopened as a bingo hall, capable of holding 250 people. This is why I believe that the original seating capacity of the theatre was about 300. The price of admission to the bingo hall was listed as 50 cents.

In 1982, the building was purchased and renovated for the Turkish Islamic Heritage Association.

BLUE BELL THEATRE (GAY)

The original plans for the Blue Bell Theatre were submitted to the city by Hubert Duerr in 1929. A neighbourhood venue that screened silent movies, its architecture was a curious mixture of shapes, the canopy over the entrance unpretentious. Located at 309 Parliament Street, on the west side of the street, it was south of Dundas Street East. Located in a working-class community, where many Irish immigrants had settled in the nineteenth century, it was in the southern part of Cabbagetown.

On January 4, 1930, a driver failed to engage his emergency brake, and his car rolled down the slight slope on Parliament Street and crashed into the ticket booth of the theatre. The cashier was too stunned to flee but fortunately was not injured, although the ticket booth was damaged.

The Blue Bell was renovated in 1933 by the architects Kaplan and Sprachman, despite being a relatively new theatre at the time. The building where the theatre was housed was a free-standing structure, with no shops included to provide extra revenues. However, it remained

Ontario Archives, RG 56-11-0-291-5

The Blue Bell Theatre, May 1946.

financially profitable for several decades. It originally contained 941 seats with leather backs. It was cooled by water-washed air.

In September 1954, the theatre was remodelled by Murray Sklar and renamed the Gay. The word was not connected with its present-day meaning. When it was renovated in 1954, the number of seats was reduced and a candy bar installed. In this year, the Gay was owned by Zelif Unger, who was well known for maintaining strict control during children's Saturday-afternoon matinees. Any kid who misbehaved was promptly ejected from the theatre. This information was obtained from a post on the Cabbagetown Regent Park Community Museum website, which also stated, "It was not uncommon [for kids] to receive a boot to the ass upon ejection." Mr. Unger sold the theatre in May 1971 for $200,000.

As the popularity of movie theatres decreased, the theatre ceased screening Hollywood films and commenced showing East Indian films. It was considered a "Bollywood" theatre and was operated by S.G.P. Jafry. The theatre finally closed during the 1980s, and today townhouses are located on the site.

CAMEO THEATRE

The Cameo Theatre was at 989 Pape Avenue, near Floyd Avenue, north of the Danforth. It is one of the theatres included in John Sebert's book *The Nabes* and is featured on the cover of his book. It was typical of the neighbourhood theatres that at one time were scattered throughout the city.

The theatre opened on November 22, 1934, during the Great Depression. Designed by Kaplan and Sprachman, it was in the Art Deco style. It resembled the Allenby Theatre on Danforth Avenue, created by the same architectural firm. At the top of the Cameo's marquee there was a small, oval-shaped design depicting the profile of a woman — a cameo. This decorative detailing gave the theatre its name.

The auditorium contained 743 seats. The façade was relatively plain, with several bold horizontal rows of bricks that were darker in colour. The bricks divided the façade into sections. The cornice was not ornate but, in typical Art Deco fashion, possessed an elevated centre section. The box office was in a central position at the edge of the sidewalk, with another decorative cameo displayed above the box-office

The Cameo Theatre in 1934.

Toronto Archives, Series 1278, File 10

window. The entrance doors were recessed a short distance from the sidewalk on Pape Avenue, and there were shops on either side of the theatre's box office.

The Cameo was the first investment project of Sam Strashin, who also operated the theatre. It remained in the possession of his family until it closed in 1957, when it was sold to Loblaws. The building still exists today, but a banking institution is located on the site.*

BAYVIEW THEATRE

The Bayview Theatre was built at 1601 Bayview Avenue by Harry Davidson and opened in 1936. The architects of the theatre were Kaplan and Sprachman, its Art Deco façade typical of their work. The 672-seat theatre was managed by Twentieth-Century Theatres.

The film on the marquee in the photo, *They Met in Bombay*, was released in 1941. It starred Clark Gable as a daring jewel thief and Rosalind Russell as a con artist.

The Bayview Theatre in 1942, showing shops on either side of its entrance.

Ontario Archives, RG 56-11-0-271-1

* The author is grateful to cinematreasures.org for some of this information.

Ontario Archives, RG 56-11-1-271

The Bayview Theatre's auditorium.

In 1943 the box office was robbed at gunpoint. The cashier refused to hand over the cash. She pushed the alarm button and the man fled. He was never apprehended. In July 1945 two women reported that they had been molested by five men who were sitting behind them. No matron was on duty when the women reported the incident, and as the men had departed, the authorities were unable to pursue the matter further.

In 1961 the Bayview ceased to operate as a movie theatre. It was renovated and reopened as the Bayview Playhouse, which showcased live theatre. The Broadway musical *Godspell* played at the Bayview for 488 performances, starring Martin Short, Eugene Levy, Dave Thomas, Andrea Martin, and Gilda Radner. The theatre closed in the late-1990s and was renovated to create several retail spaces.

BIRCHCLIFF THEATRE

Judging by comments posted on the internet, many people retain fond memories of their youth in the Birch Cliff community of East Toronto, and of the Birchcliff Theatre in particular. Because I grew up in the west end of Toronto, I was never in this theatre, but I can certainly relate to the comments posted online about the Saturday afternoon matinees at the Birchcliff and the memories created by some of the great films screened within it during the 1950s and 1960s.

The theatre was built in 1949, in the days when Birch Cliff was a quiet neighbourhood where people knew each other, and there were street parties and other community events. Birch Cliff was within walking distance of Lake Ontario, so it was an ideal neighbourhood for a kid to grow up in. Many considered the Birchcliff Theatre the "icing on the cake" that made growing up in the community so special.

The theatre was built on the site of an old streetcar barn, located at 1535 Kingston Road, on the south side of the street, near Warden

Ontario Archives, RG 56-11-0-272-1

The Birchcliff Theatre in 1949.

Avenue. It was part of the Twentieth-Century Theatre chain, owned by Nat Taylor. In later years, Nat Taylor owned Loew's Uptown, and in 1979 he partnered with Garth Drabinsky to build the Odeon Cineplex Eaton Centre, the largest multi-screen theatre complex in the world at that time.

The Birchcliff Theatre was typical of theatres built after the Second World War. Its architecture could be referred to as ranch-style, although this was a term usually applied to homes constructed in the suburbs in the postwar period. The theatres in this style were one storey in height, built with brick and concrete, often having large surfaces of concrete, glass, or granite. Their large windows permitted generous amounts of daylight into the lobbies, allowing them to be viewed from outside.

In many ways, the Birchcliff's architecture was akin to that of the Nortown on Eglinton Avenue West, although the latter theatre was more upscale. The Birchcliff was also similar to the University on Bloor Street, although the University was more impressive than even the Nortown. However, the theatre that perhaps most resembled the Birchcliff was the Westwood near Six Points, in the west end of the city. It was boxy and composed of basic rectangular shapes.

The Birchcliff screened films until 1974, when television diminished attendance to the extent that it became unprofitable. After the theatre closed it was demolished, and today there is an ambulance service on the site — Toronto Emergency Medical Services.

GOLDEN MILE THEATRE

The Golden Mile Theatre, located in Scarborough at 1816 Eglinton Avenue East, opened on October 14, 1954. It architecturally resembled other postwar theatres and in many ways was similar to the Birchcliff. The Golden Mile offered spacious parking in an era when automobile sales were booming.

The theatre was located in the Golden Mile Plaza, on the northeast corner of the intersection of Eglinton Avenue East and Victoria Park. It was licensed to West Pen Theatres Limited, but owned by Principal Investments. The name "Golden Mile" referred to a section of Eglinton

The Golden Mile Theatre in 1954. The TTC Express Bus transported fans directly to Maple Leaf Gardens for hockey games.

East, between Pharmacy and Birchmount Avenues, where there was a concentration of million-dollar industries. The Golden Mile Theatre was the first theatre constructed in Canada in a shopping mall, which provided spacious parking for cars. This concept spread quickly across the nation. It appealed to those who lived in the suburbs, as they were able to park, shop, visit a restaurant, and attend a movie all in a single location.

The Golden Mile Theatre specialized in films aimed toward families. It opened on October 14, 1954, a year when television was already eroding the popularity of neighbourhood theatres. It contained approximately a thousand seats, which were plush and "self-rising." There were 720 on the ground floor and another 275 in the balcony. The total cost of construction and furnishings was $310,000. The air-conditioned interior was ultra-modern, decorated with marble and glass.

On the opening night, one of the films was *Up in Arms*, released in 1944, starring Danny Kaye. The other movie was *Our Very Own*, released in 1950, starring Ann Blyth. Neither of the films was a recent release, but both were suitable for family viewing. The theatre was open during evenings only, except on Saturday when there were children's matinees.

In 1957, during a matinee with 350 children in attendance, there was a fire in the air-conditioning system. The theatre was evacuated within three and a half minutes. The damage was minimal and the theatre opened again in the evening.

In 1959, Queen Elizabeth II visited the Golden Mile Plaza, as city officials wished to highlight the city's newest attraction. Strip malls eventually fell out of favour, as indoor malls such as Yorkdale were built. Today, high-end strip malls are making a comeback, as witnessed in Don Mills.

In 1978 the Golden Mile Theatre was divided into two auditoriums by the architects Mandel Sprachman, who also designed the plans for the conversion of the Uptown and the Imperial Theatres into multiplex theatres. The theatre remained active until the mid-1980s.

Although the theatre and the shopping plaza where it was located have now disappeared, they live on in the memory of those who visited the plaza and those who attended this fine suburban theatre.

CHAPTER SIX

Theatres West of Yonge Street, on Queen Street West

PICKFORD THEATRE (AUDITORIUM, AVENUE, VARIETY)

The intersection of Spadina Avenue and Queen Street West is today one of the busiest intersections in downtown Toronto. I sometimes refer to it as "hamburger corner," as there are four fast-food hamburger outlets located near this intersection. However, until I commenced researching Toronto's old movie houses, I had never realized that it was also the site of one of the city's earliest theatres — the Auditorium Theatre.

It was located at 382 Queen Street West, on the northwest corner of Spadina Avenue and Queen Street West. It opened in 1908, on the ground-floor level of the Moler College Barber Building, which was three-storeys high and topped by a mansard roof. A 1935 photo depicts the theatre and shows two of the three storeys above it.

When the Auditorium opened in the first decade of the twentieth century, the movie theatre business was in its infancy and considered a risky enterprise. Thus, renting space within an existing building was the least expensive way to present "photo plays," as they then called movies. However, within a few years this attitude changed due to the increasing popularity of films. Buildings were then constructed for the sole purpose of showing motion pictures. The situation was reversed, as the theatre owners rented excess space to other businesses. The funds assisted in reducing the expenses of operating a theatre.

The Standard Theatre c. 1910, as the film The Heroine of Mafeking *was released in 1909.*

The intersection of Queen Street West and Spadina Avenue, looking north. The Pickford Theatre was on the ground floor of the building to the left.

When the Auditorium opened, it imitated the format of the Theatorium Theatre at Yonge and Queen, which featured films and a series of vaudeville acts. The Theatorium was called a nickelodeon, as it charged 5 cents for tickets. The Auditorium Theatre followed this pattern, boasting that it showed films that required three reels to complete, considered quite a technological feat in 1908.

The interior space of the theatre was long and narrow, extending back from Queen Street. There was a stage at the north end of the auditorium, but its ceiling was not of sufficient height to accommodate a large screen. This restriction also prevented the theatre from having a balcony. Thus, it was a small theatre, containing fewer than 400 leatherette seats, all with plush backs. From its opening day in 1908, it was well attended as there were no other theatres in close proximity.

In 1913 the theatre was renovated. Its north wall was extended further back to increase the seating capacity by almost fifty seats. Following the alterations, the theatre was renamed the Avenue, the name likely chosen because it was located on one of the city's grand avenues — Spadina Avenue.

In 1915 the name was again changed, becoming the Mary Pickford Theatre in order to take advantage of the fame associated with the first true international film star of the silver screen. Pickford had been born in Toronto, and her name added to the popularity of the theatre. The theatre's name was later shortened and it was simply referred to as the Pickford. This name was to remain until 1945, when it was renamed the Variety.

The old theatre finally closed in 1947. The Moler Barber Building, where the Pickford had been located, was then occupied by Bargain Benny's, which was similar to Honest Ed's. Bargain Benny's went bankrupt in 1961. After the building was demolished in 1972, a small café was erected on the site. Today a McDonald's occupies the corner.

RIVOLI THEATRE (PEOPLE'S)

In the summer of 2013, I saw a temporary plaque in the window of the Rivoli Restaurant at 334 Queen Street West giving the history of the building. I had passed the Rivoli many times, but never realized that the site had once housed one of the city's earliest vaudeville and burlesque houses, as well as a silent movie theatre.

Information on this theatre was almost nonexistent, and I discovered no photographs in the archives. However, I was fortunate that Colby Bayne forwarded to me a misfiled photo that he had discovered in the Toronto Archives. It is likely the only picture that exists of this old movie house. To supplement the details evident in the photo, I examined the structure in detail and theorized how the building that contained the Rivoli might have looked when it was a functioning theatre.

According to information researched by Paul Moore, of the Canadian Theatre Historical Project at Ryerson University, the theatre opened in

The Rivoli Restaurant and Club on Queen Street West a short distance east of Spadina, taken in 2014.

January 1911. The theatre was originally named the People's Theatre, but in 1925 its name was changed to the Rivoli. The name was derived from a town in Italy in the province of Verona. I was unable to find any details about the theatre's interior.

Today, the Edwardian building has a symmetrical façade and possesses very little ornamentation. Almost all the architectural detailing from the days when it was a theatre has disappeared. The roof of the building has also been altered. Originally, it likely possessed a sloped roof, with large chimneys. Today, the roof is flat and there are no chimneys in evidence.

When the People's Theatre opened in 1911, the concept of constructing buildings specifically for screening "moving pictures" was in its infancy. The Colonial Theatre, later renamed the Bay, opened in 1909 and was the first structure in Toronto built solely for screening films.

The strip of Queen Street West where the Rivoli was located contained houses as early as the 1850s. These were demolished in the 1870s and 1880s to construct shops with three or four storeys with residential apartments above. The People's Theatre opened in the shop on the ground floor of 334 Queen West.

Because the theatre occupied the first-floor level only, it is extremely unlikely that it possessed a balcony and there would not have been many seats. The projection screen at the north end of the auditorium was not large, as it was limited by the height of the ceiling.

The surviving photo of the theatre reveals that in the early years of the twentieth century the theatre's box office was inside the lobby. The canopy over the entrance was a plain rectangular shape, with scalloped edges. Posters advertising the current films, as well as future attractions, were displayed in billboards on either side of the entrance.

When the People's opened in 1911, its major competitor was the Auditorium Theatre (the Pickford), on the northwest corner of Spadina and Queen.

In 1982, the building that had housed the Rivoli Theatre was renovated and opened as a trendy restaurant and club. It helped define Queen Street West as a street that was funky, outlandish, and hip. The Canadian group Blue Rodeo first performed in the club in the back room

This photograph is of Leo Turofsky on the occasion of the purchase of his first automobile. The two men in the car dominate the picture, but the Rivoli is visible in the background. All of the buildings in the photo remain on Queen Street West in 2016. The florist shop to the west of the theatre is People's Florists. Perhaps it had the same owners as the theatre.

in February 1985, just a year after the group was formed. *The Drowsy Chaperone*, a spoof of 1920s musicals, debuted at the Rivoli in 1998. It became a hit when staged at Toronto's Fringe Festival, and in 2001 was part of the Mirvish subscription series. Its success led to its opening on Broadway on May 1, 2006.

Today, the Rivoli restaurant and club remain popular and are well-known on the Queen West strip. However, no traces of the old theatre from 1911 remain, other than the name that the theatre was given in 1925.

AVON THEATRE
(CHILD'S, KING'S HALL, KING'S PLAYHOUSE)

The restored building at 1092 Queen Street West once housed the Avon Theatre. When I moved from the suburbs to downtown in 2000, the marquee above the doorway remained from the days when the building was the site of a 325-seat movie theatre. The marquee stayed up

Left: *The site of the Avon Theatre in 2015.*

Below: *The Avon Theatre in July 1955.*

Toronto Archives, Series 1278, File 10

until Starbucks Coffee restored the building. It is a handsome structure, with its red-brick façades, stone, and cement trim. Its mansard roof has gabled windows.

The building was constructed in 1887. In that year there was a fruit market on the ground floor, with apartments above it. It remained a retail outlet until 1915, when Child's Theatre opened on the premises. This theatre lasted only a year, and then it became King's Hall and King's Playhouse Theatre, operated by Mr. King Hyman. In 1950 it became the Avon Theatre.

ODEON THEATRE

The Odeon Theatre at 1558 Queen Street West was in the former village of Parkdale, which was annexed to the city in 1889. The theatre opened in 1919, a year after the end of the First World War. A night at the movies provided a welcome relief to the war-weary people of the community, providing an evening's entertainment and an opportunity to forget the horrors of the casualty reports from previous years.

The Odeon had no connection to the British Odeon Theatre Company that began building theatres in the city in the 1940s. The word *Odeon* is derived from the name of an ancient Greek theatre, the Odeon of Herodes Atticus, in Athens, built between 160 and 174 A.D. Located on the south side of the Acropolis, the theatre still exists today.

The two-storey red-brick building had a residential apartment on the second floor. Its symmetrical façade was formal and dignified, the stone trim adding architectural detail. The cornice was plain, with a narrow parapet to create the illusion of extra height if viewed from a distance.

The theatre's auditorium possessed two aisles, with a centre section and aisles on either side. There were no side aisles, meaning that seats were adjacent to the side walls. It had a sloped floor extending from where the screen was located to the rear wall, the back rows accessed by stairs. The auditorium walls were plain with very few decorative details, although there were attractive designs surrounding the screen.

Left: *The Odeon Theatre in 1919. The featured movie is Cecil B. DeMille's* Don't Change Your Husband, *a silent comedy released in 1919.*

Below: *The site of the Odeon Theatre as it appeared in 2014.*

A letter in the files at the Toronto Archives confirms that the theatre closed in October 1968. However, the building remains on Queen Street today and contains a fruit market.

KUM-C THEATRE

I was unable to discover the exact year that the KUM-C Theatre opened, but according to John Sebert's book *The Nabes*, it originally screened silent movies and featured vaudeville. This means that it was in operation prior to the introduction of the "talkies." One source states that the KUM-C Theatre opened in 1919, the year before the Parkdale Theatre. The Parkdale, which was the KUM-C's rival, was located further west along Queen Street. However, the Parkdale was a much larger and classier theatre, which originally screened recently released films. The KUM-C showed movies that were a year or two old.

The KUM-C was located at 1288 Queen Street West, on the eastern edge of the community of Parkdale. It was on the north side of Queen, one block west of Dufferin Street. I did not find any reference to the source of its name, but I assume that it was a play on the words "Come See." Whoever named the theatre had a tongue-in-cheek sense of humour. I doubt that anyone today would choose such a name. Pity!

When the theatre opened, it was only half the size of the theatre shown in the 1935 photo. The original brick building that housed the theatre was set back a short distance from the sidewalk. It possessed a rather plain façade of stucco over brick, with an unadorned cornice. There were two large rectangular windows on the second floor that had rounded edges at the top. As was the case with most theatres in the early decades of the twentieth century, the second storey contained apartments that provided rental income for the owner of the theatre. There was no air-conditioning, but it possessed a vent and a roof fan. The auditorium contained only one aisle, positioned in the centre.

In 1930, the theatre was extensively renovated by Kaplan and Sprachman. Their architectural sketch, dated June 1930, shows the theatre's planned alterations. It was still only half the size of what it later

City of Toronto Archives, Series 1278, File 10

The KUM-C Theatre c. 1935. The admission prices advertised on the marquee are indeed a bargain by modern standards.

became. However, the front of the theatre was extended to the edge of the sidewalk and the box office relocated to a central position, with French doors on either side.

I was unable to discover when the owners of the KUM-C purchased the store to the east to extend the theatre. One note in the Toronto Archive's files states that this occurred in 1930, but the sketch by Kaplan and Sprachman seems to contradict this information. However, it is known that after the theatre was enlarged it contained almost 600 seats, with leatherette bottoms and wooden backs. There were also fourteen extra folding chairs that were employed when the theatre was at capacity. The floor of the auditorium was concrete.

On February 24, 1943, the theatre's manager was reprimanded by the chief inspector of theatres for allowing the screening to extend beyond the midnight hour. Another infraction occurred on November 6, 1943, when an inspector in an automobile parked across from the theatre observed nine children under sixteen years of age entering, unaccompanied by an adult. The following day, the same inspector saw the theatre's matron sitting in the audience watching the film, and she was not in uniform. The inspector forcefully reminded the theatre's manager that the matron's job was to circulate up and down the aisles and be evident at all times. When he returned the next day to see if his warning had been heeded, he discovered that the matron was indeed visible, but her uniform was old and it was the wrong size. The manager assured the inspector that a new uniform had been ordered.

In April 1947, a candy bar was installed at the KUM-C.

On December 21, 1957, the theatre was again in trouble. It was found that three of the fire doors had been bolted shut with wooden planks during a children's matinee. The manager was summonsed to appear in court, found guilty, and fined $50.

In 1961, the theatre was listed on the real estate market at the asking price of $68,500. The ad stated that the taxes were $9,600, the heating costs were $300 annually, and the insurance was $100. It is assumed that

The site of the KUM-C Theatre at 1288 Queen Street West in Parkdale. In 2016 the building is painted flaming red. The windows on the second floor have been modernized. The building to the east of the theatre's site has disappeared.

this was when Nat Taylor of Twentieth-Century Theatres purchased it, as the files state that he owned the theatre during the 1960s. The theatre ceased screening films about 1970. However, as late as 1973 it remained empty and was for sale for $175,000. The building was eventually purchased and renovated for other commercial purposes.

PARKDALE THEATRE

The Parkdale Theatre at 1605 Queen Street West, on the northwest corner of Queen and Triller Avenue, is another of Toronto's theatres that I can readily recall, though I never was inside its doors. As a child in the 1940s, I often gazed at its showy marquee from the windows of the Queen streetcars on our way to Sunnyside Beach for a day beside the lake. The theatre was only one city block away from the "three-way corner" of Queen, Roncesvalles, and King Street West. We alighted from the streetcar at this intersection, crossed a narrow bridge spanning the railway tracks, and descended the stairs to the amusement park and beach, located on Lakeshore Boulevard.

City of Toronto Archives, Series 881- file 350

Parkdale Theatre in 1937.

I also remember that at the three-way corner, on the northwest corner, there was a Gray Coach Bus Terminal, and next to it was the Edgewater Hotel. The Parkdale Theatre was only a short walk from these well-known city landmarks. All these buildings remain in 2016, but have been converted for other commercial purposes.

In the first decade of the twentieth century, as Toronto's population crept westward, Parkdale's population expanded. Prior to the First World War, construction commenced at Sunnyside to extend the beach and create an amusement park. The work ceased during the war and continued after it ended. As it neared completion, it was obvious that the area would be ideal for movie theatres. The opportunity was seized by the Allen brothers, Jule and Jay, who already owned the Allen Theatre (Tivoli) at Adelaide and Victoria Streets and the Allen's Danforth.

The Parkdale opened on April 5, 1920, in time for the summer season. It was designed by Howard Crane of Detroit. The theatre was a large rectangular yellow-brick building, its auditorium built parallel to Queen Street. Its façade was relatively plain, except for stone detailing below the cornice. However, the interior of the Parkdale was luxurious, typical of most Allen theatres. Patrons were astonished at the gilded patterns and fancy plaster trim throughout the theatre. The ceiling was the equivalent of three storeys in height, containing well-crafted designs with enormous concentric rings and a large medallion in the centre. Striking decorative lines radiated from the central medallion. Chandeliers were suspended from this ornate ceiling, and below them were 1,500 seats with leather bottoms and backs. Four wide aisles allowed easy access and departures from the rows. The entrance lobby was equally impressive, with Wedgewood-style designs above the entrance doors and those leading into the auditorium.

In January 1938 water-washed air conditioning was installed. It was not until 1950 that a candy bar was added. Today, this seems quite strange, as modern theatres derive a high percentage of their revenues from popcorn, drinks, and other treats. Even stranger, after the candy bar was installed, the sale of popcorn was not allowed, as it was considered too messy.

In the early 1950s, the Parkdale screened NHL games. This was in the years when theatres were not able to legally screen films on Sundays and no Sunday sports were allowed. The broadcasts at the Parkdale

Ontario Archives, RG 56-11-0-312-3

Auditorium of the Parkdale.

originated from one of the four American cities in a league that in those years had only six teams. Coverage of the NHL home games was confined to the radio, so viewing hockey games on the theatre's big screen was very popular. This information was obtained from Barry Long of Oakville, who attended the broadcasts at the Parkdale when he was boy.

Despite its original opulence, as the years progressed the Parkdale slowly lost in the competition with television. The theatre closed on July 6, 1970. The building on Queen Street in Parkdale remains today, but has been converted into shops that specialize in second-hand and antique furniture.

ORPHEUM THEATRE (ROSEMARY, GOLDEN DRAGON)

The building that once housed the old Orpheum Theatre, at 600–602 Queen Street West, still stands in 2016. The marquee above the doorway still protects customers from rain or snow, and in summer it shields

City of Toronto Archives, Series 1278, File 10

This photo of the Orpheum was taken after 1961, as the theatre is offering Sunday matinees. Prior to this date, screening films on Sundays was illegal. The camera is pointed east on Queen Street West toward Bathurst Street.

them from the heat of the afternoon sun. The two bank buildings on the corners of Bathurst and Queen, visible in the photo, also remain today. However, since the area along Queen West is changing rapidly, I fear for the future of the structure where the Orpheum was once located.

This building began its life in 1912, when it contained the George Dodds Amusement Arcade. In 1930, it was renovated to house the Orpheum Theatre, as the large space occupied by the amusement arcade was an ideal space for a theatre. The year before the theatre opened, the Great Depression descended on Toronto, but attending the movies remained highly popular.

The theatre contained two aisles, with almost 500 plush seats with well-padded backs. In the balcony there were another 146 seats. The ladies' washroom was accessed from the right-hand side of the lobby, but the men's was in the basement. The façade was renovated by Jay English in 1940. It is this façade that survives to this day. A candy bar was installed in December 1950, placed behind the back row of the centre section of seats.

The following is from an email I received from Larry Rittenberg, grandson of the orginal owner: "The Orpheum Theatre was opened by my grandfather Norman, and subsequently owned by my father, Morris, and his brother-in-law Percy (also the projectionist) until it closed. I helped out there on the candy bar on Saturday matinees."

Orpheum Theatre continued to screen films for over forty years. During its later years, patrons were able to call the number EM 8-5752 to discover the starting times of the films. However, the Orpheum slowly lost the battle and closed its doors in 1977. It was vacant for two years, but in 1980 it reopened as the Rosemary Theatre. This theatre lasted two years more.

In 1983, it was renamed the Golden Dragon, screening Asian movies. The theatre was closed permanently in 1987 and became a jewellery store. It has since been occupied by various companies, but the marquee over the door remains to this day.

CHAPTER SEVEN

Theatres on Dundas Street West

BEAVER THEATRE

In the nineteenth century, the district that became known as the Junction was a rural farming community to the northwest of Toronto. It centred upon Keele and Dundas Street West. The name "Junction" was derived from the fact that it was at the junction of four railway lines. The southern terminal of the old Weston Road streetcars, which travelled north to the town of Weston, was also at the Junction. The West Toronto Railway Station was on the east side of Keele Street, several blocks north of Dundas. The old stone railway bridge remains in use today and continues to span Keele Street, although the railway station was demolished decades ago.

As the twentieth century dawned, because the Junction was a transportation hub, more and more people built homes in the area. It eventually developed into the town of West Toronto, which was annexed to the city in 1909. With the increase in population, more businesses gravitated to the area. It was not long before it was realized that the town needed a movie theatre.

The man who fulfilled this need was William Joy. In 1907, he had opened a small theatre named the Wonderland, which featured live performances. It was a profitable enterprise. In 1913 he closed the Wonderland and opened the Beaver Theatre, at a cost of $60,000. His new theatre was

The Beaver Theatre in 1947. The cowboy film starring Gene Autry received top billing over the George Sanders film The Private Affairs of Bel Amit.

City of Toronto Archives, Series 1278, File 63

to show moving pictures and feature vaudeville acts. He managed the new theatre himself. He also insisted that the Beaver have a fire-proof picture curtain and personally supervised its installation.

The Beaver was located at 2942 Dundas Street West, near Pacific Avenue. It was an impressive structure, especially considering that in those days it was remote from downtown Toronto, where the demographics provided more possibilities for patrons. The Beaver's architect was Neil G. Beggs, and the neoclassical façade that he created was quite ornate. Its symmetrical design included an ornamented cornice, with an impressive row of dentils below it. The façade contained smooth, glossy terracotta tiles glazed with a light-yellow patina. The lower lobby and foyer possessed alternate mirrored panels with frames of terracotta and rouge-noir marble.

The theatre auditorium's colour scheme was antique ivory and green, and on the ceiling was a large mural of flying cupids. The seating capacity was approximately 800, including a narrow balcony that was 50 by 176 feet, decorated with bronze of various shades. There were box seats along the sides of the auditorium, those closest to the stage less than 50 feet from the actors.

In 1918, the theatre was taken over by the Allen brothers, who owned Allen's Danforth and the Allen Theatre at Adelaide and Victoria. In later years, the Beaver Theatre was operated by the B&F chain. This company renovated and modernized it. The box seats were removed, as by that time the theatre was exclusively employed for movies.

In 1961 the Beaver closed — one of the first to succumb to television.

DUCHESS THEATRE (CENTRE)

Plans for the Duchess Theatre were submitted to the City of Toronto in December 1914. It was located at 20–22 Arthur Street, on the corner of Arthur and Markham. In those years, Bloor and Queen Streets were the only major east-west streets crossing the city, and it was evident that another street was required to facilitate traffic flow. Dundas Street was created by stitching together various east-west streets, Arthur Street being one of them. When Dundas Street was created, the address of the Duchess Theatre changed from 20–22 Arthur Street to 722 Dundas Street West. It was a small theatre, with 469 wooden seats on a concrete floor, with no balcony.

In 1929, the theatre was renovated and the seating increased to 505 upholstered seats. The building was two storeys high, its brick façade and cornice unadorned. The Duchess was renovated again in 1940, the plans designed by Jay English. It is likely that this is when its name was changed to the Centre Theatre.

In 1947, there were complaints that kids in the theatre were rowdy and flagrantly smoking. One complainant wrote: "The teenagers were in the theatre for purposes other than observing the picture." The writer did not state the teenagers' true purposes, so it is left to our imagination.

The Centre Theatre c. 1944.

By 1948, the theatre had seriously deteriorated. A patron reported to officials that it was not heated in the evenings, there was smoking throughout the theatre, seats were broken, and kids were wildly running up and down the aisles. As well, there was profane language and the teenagers were partly nude. The person who reported this state of affairs said that she had intended to write to the magazine *Hush*. However, upon reflection, instead she sent a letter to Mayor Saunders, who forwarded the letter to the Picture Censors. I remember *Hush* magazine quite well. Its motto was "All the news that's fit to print." It was Toronto's most popular "slush" magazine in the 1940s and 1950s.

I suppose I should confess that my name appeared in *Hush* magazine on one occasion in the early 1950s. I was passed a forged cheque by a customer of Crosstown Pharmacy when I was a delivery boy for the drug store. I went to court to identify the man. My name was published in *Hush* in reference to the court case. I brought the newspaper home to show my parents, but my mother threw it out before I had a chance to explain why I was in possession of such a "filthy newspaper," as she referred to it. My one and only opportunity to achieve boyhood notoriety went into the garbage.

In September 1957, it was discovered that the fire doors of the Centre Theatre were locked. In court, the manager said that the theatre had been broken into several times and the safe stolen. The fine for the offence of locking the fire doors was between $50 and $500. The judge fined the theatre manager $75.

I was unable to verify the year when the Centre Theatre closed.

APOLLO (CRYSTAL)

Unfortunately, the Apollo Theatre disappeared long ago. It was located at 2901 Dundas Street West, in the Junction area of Toronto's west end. It was on the south side of the street, near the corner of Mavety, one block west of Keele Street, in a building with shops on the ground floor and apartments and offices on the second and third floors

The Toronto Directories reveal that in 1921 there was a second-floor apartment rented by Sarah Ford, which also contained Robert J. Bruce Amusements. The following year Sarah Ford's name is still listed, but the amusement company had disappeared and the apartment contained the Crystal Theatre. I thought that perhaps the second-floor location was the offices for the theatre, but there is no theatre listed as being on the ground floor.

Not until 1931 did the directories indicate that the Crystal Theatre was on the first floor, with the postal address of 2901 Dundas Street West. However, a 1922 photo seems to contradict this information, as it shows a large canopy extending over the sidewalk with the words *Crystal Theatre* on it. I suppose it's possible that the canopy was for the theatre on the second floor, but this seems unlikely. It is also possible that the date on the photo in the archives is incorrect.

The Crystal was a small neighbourhood theatre that competed with the more upscale Beaver Theatre, which had opened in 1907 on Dundas Street West. Records indicate that the Crystal contained 562

City of Toronto Archives, Series 1278, File 56

The Apollo Theatre on Dundas Street West.

wood seats in an auditorium that was narrow, stretching back a considerable distance from the street. There was no balcony, but the theatre possessed a stage. Similar to other theatres in this decade, it offered live performances and vaudeville, as well as the screenings of silent movies. Sound films had already arrived in Toronto, but because the Crystal was a small neighbourhood venue, it was unlikely that it had converted to the new technology. The theatre's box office was close to the sidewalk, in a central position.

In 1934 its name was changed to the Apollo, and by this year the theatre was likely screening sound films. The Apollo was just one of several theatres located on Dundas Street West in the Junction area of the city.

LA SALLE THEATRE (LIBERTY, PAGODA)

The 1953 photo of the La Salle Theatre is the only one that I was able to locate in the archives. It is fortunate that someone took this picture of a fire engine parked on Dundas Street West on a spring afternoon in 1953.

The La Salle Theatre in 1953. The bank to the east of the theatre rented space within its building to a small variety store.

City of Toronto Archives, Salmon Collection, Series 1278, File 10

The fire truck had been called to extinguish a fire at M. Mandel and Sons Lumber Yard, on the west side of Spadina Avenue, north of Dundas Street.

The La Salle Theatre opened in 1928 and was originally named the Liberty; it was licensed to Mr. A. Finkelstein. Located at 526–528 Dundas Street West, on the north side of the street, immediately to the west of a branch of the Bank of Nova Scotia, on the northwest corner of Dundas and Spadina. The building where the theatre was located survives to 2016, as well as the bank. The bank remains an active branch, but the theatre disappeared decades ago. The two building are separated by a narrow alley, which also remains.

The theatre possessed a floor of concrete and steel, with 450 seats in its auditorium and another 200 in the balcony. The ladies' room was to the right of the foyer and the men's room was in the basement. This arrangement was typical for washrooms in decades past. The theatre was cooled by water-washed air, installed by the Canadian Air Conditioning Company.

In 1938 the theatre was renovated, the plans designed by Harry Dobson, and its name changed from the Liberty to the La Salle. In 1940 an inspector reported that the theatre was not being maintained properly and that the owner was uncooperative. A similar report was issued the following year, and again in 1943 and 1944. An inspector also noted that although the matron on duty at the La Salle was wearing the mandatory white uniform, the word *matron* was missing. Apparently, this was a mandatory requirement for all matrons' uniforms. This information in the file of the La Salle Theatre in the archives is the first time I have seen this requirement stipulated.

During the 1960s, because of the demographic changes in the Spadina/Dundas area, the theatre screened Chinese films and its name was changed to the Pagoda. The theatre finally closed in the late 1960s or early 1970s. The latter information was obtained from Carlos De Sousa, who lived on Kensington Avenue in the 1960s and often attended the theatre.

The building at 526–528 Dundas West, site of the old La Salle Theatre. The space occupied by the variety shop in the earlier photo is now incorporated into the bank (2015).

Because I often shop in Kensington Market, I have passed the building where the La Salle was located many times but was unaware that a theatre had been located on the site. After my research, I re-examined the building and for the first time realized that the shape of the structure resembled a theatre.

ROYAL THEATRE (ROMA)

When the harsh economic times that became known as the Great Depression descended across the city, unemployment soared and food lines became lengthy. People possessed very few dollars to spend, but movies were relatively cheap and readily available in almost every neighbourhood, so theatres continued to be built. Plans for the Royal Theatre, to be located at 1481–83 Dundas Street West, on the northwest corner of Dufferin and Dundas Streets, were submitted to the city in March 1930.

Determining if the Royal was located in a building that was constructed as a theatre or occupied a space that had formerly been a store was difficult. The latter is the more likely, since the architectural style

The Royal Theatre c. 1948.

City of Toronto Archives, Series 1278, File 10

of the building resembled the 1920s more than the 1930s. The building contained a symmetrical parapet at the top, with a plain cornice. The structure extended a considerable distance back from Dundas Street, which allowed space for seven residential apartments on the second floor. The apartments had attractive bay windows and a separate entrance on Dufferin Street. The Royal's auditorium possessed a concrete floor, with 366 leatherette seats with plush backs, but no balcony. Its small size also suggests that it was in a converted space rather than in a location purposely built as a theatre.

Around 1953, due to demographic changes in the area, the theatre changed its name to the Roma and screened Italian films. In June 1955, the building was listed on the real estate market. However, I was unable to discover the year that the Royal was purchased or when it closed.

After its demise, the Pylon Theatre on College Street, which had been renamed the Golden Princess when it screened Asian films, took the name Royal as its own. The Royal at 608–610 College Streets remains in Little Italy and is a vibrant part of the community.

BROCK THEATRE (DUNDAS PLAYHOUSE, GEM)

The Brock Theatre at 1587 Dundas Street West opened in 1936. It was between Lansdowne Avenue and Dufferin Street, east of Brock Avenue. The two-storey building was originally the Dundas Playhouse, but was renovated by Sprachman and Mandel and reopened in 1936 as the Brock Theatre, owned by Samuel Lent.

The Brock contained 706 seats, all on one level, as there was no balcony. The façade was exceedingly plain, typical of many buildings erected during the Great Depression. However, the canopy over the entrance was extravagant and attracted attention at the street level, especially when its lights flashed in the darkness of a moonless evening.

Unfortunately, moonless evenings were ideal for those with criminal intent. In February 1949, a man with a nylon stocking over his head pushed his arm through the window of the box office and punched the stomach of the young girl selling tickets. The robber waved a revolver

Brock Theatre on Dundas West in 1937. The film Ebb Tide, *starring Ray Milland, is advertised on the marquee.*

in her face, but instead of handing over the cash she pushed the alarm buzzer. The manager immediately rushed to the scene, and the man fled.

The same year as the attempted robbery the theatre was again renovated by Sprachman and Mandel, and its name was changed to the Gem. During these renovations the old marquee was removed. The new marquee was smaller and v-shaped, with the word *Gem* on either side of it. Gem also appeared on the top of the marquee in large letters. A candy bar was also added during these renovations.

The theatre was again updated in 1955 and for a brief period screened Italian films, and then Polish. However, attendance declined, and in 1958 its owners listed the theatre on the real estate market for an asking price of $65,000. It was listed again in January 1961, but the price was reduced to $55,000. In May 1961 it was reduced to $33,500. The theatre eventually closed and the premises were renovated to create a banquet hall. In January 1965, the site of the old Brock Theatre was again on the market at the asking price of $120,000.

CHAPTER EIGHT

Theatres on College and Carlton Streets

KING THEATRE (KINO, STUDIO)

The plans for the King Theatre were submitted to the City of Toronto in December 1914, shortly after the outbreak of the First World War. The King contained 347 seats, with a centre aisle only, as the theatre was too narrow to accommodate a second aisle. Because of the auditorium's extreme length, the back rows were a considerable distance from the stage and screen. The rows of seats on the left-hand (east) side of the aisle were interrupted in two places to provide emergency exits, similar to the bulkhead seats on airplanes today. Located at 565 College Street, it was on the southwest corner at Manning Street. Vaudeville and silent movies were both featured.

In January 1930 a fire occurred in the projection room, which was tucked behind one of the apartments on the second floor. The flames were quickly extinguished by the manager, who employed a "chemical fire apparatus," as the newspapers referred to it (a fire extinguisher). However, because the fire department had been called, firemen arrived and entered the theatre by a side door to avoid alarming those attending the show. Fortunately, there was no need for their services as the fire had already been put out. The fire occurred during a matinee, when there were mostly children in the theatre. They were not aware that anything had occurred, as there was only a short break in the screening.

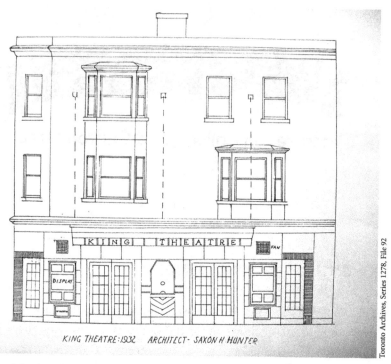

KING THEATRE:1932   ARCHITECT- SAXON H HUNTER

Sketch of the façade of the King Theatre for the renovations in 1932, by the architect Saxon H. Hunter.

In 1932 there were major alterations to the King Theatre, employing plans designed by Saxon H. Hunter, who was also the architect of the Family Theatre on Queen Street East.

Essentially, Saxon rebuilt the theatre, since land had been purchased to allow the auditorium of the theatre to be widened. This meant designing a new façade. The renovated auditorium had two aisles, and the seating capacity was increased to approximately 600 seats. The apartments above the theatre were enlarged. On the second floor, one of the apartments was where the theatre's owner resided. On the third floor, the more spacious apartment had several bedrooms.

On November 27, 1933, the manager of the theatre, George A. Lester, was badly beaten while inside the theatre. Two men from Detroit were arrested for the crime on December 5th. They said that they had been hired as "muscle men" by a rival theatre owner and paid $50 each.

Because they were contacted by a go-between, the person who placed the contract was never identified. It was said that the improvements to the King Theatre in 1932 had increased the King's business to the detriment of the other theatres in the area and this was the reason for the mugging.

In 1942, the King Theatre's licence was transferred from Angel Lester to Odeon Theatres.

In September 1946 the theatre was purchased by Norman Clavir from the Odeon Corporation. He changed the name of the theatre to the Kino and specialized in foreign films. It was the second theatre in Toronto to adopt this format, the other being the International Cinema. The first foreign film screened at the Kino was *Russia on Parade* and the second film was *Hello Moscow!*; both of them were Artkino Pictures productions. At the same time, the International Cinema was showing *Henry V*

Ontario Archives, RG 56-11-0-320-1

Marquee and entrance of the King Theatre c. 1942. The Gay Sisters was one of the featured films.

with Laurence Olivier. In 1948 or 1949 the theatre's name reverted again to the King, but it continued to screen foreign films.

A letter dated September 24, 1951, indicates that the name of the theatre was changed to the Studio. The same year, the theatre was again under renovation, this time according to plans created by Kaplan and Sprachman. A candy bar that sold popcorn was added to the right-hand side of the foyer.

Inspectors' reports continued to be filed until 1969, and then they ceased. It is assumed that this was the year that the theatre closed. The theatre was demolished and a three-storey office building constructed on the site.

GARDEN THEATRE (CINEMA LUMIERE)

The Garden Theatre was among the first of the city's movie houses. Plans were submitted to the City of Toronto for the site at 290 College in March 1915, proposing that two shops be combined into a single space to house Leon Brick's Amusement Arcade. The plans were approved and a rooftop garden, designed by J.H. Stanford, was built on top of the structure.

In 1916 the premises changed hands and were converted into the Garden Theatre, but the roof garden was retained. The open-air space contained chairs and tables, arranged for patrons to enjoy refreshments. The theatre below the roof garden contained 481 leatherette seats in the auditorium and another fifty-seven wooden seats in the small balcony. The theatre possessed no air-conditioning, but had fans and vents to circulate the air.

In 1936 the owners hired Kaplan and Sprachman to renovate. The floor of the auditorium was changed from wood to concrete and the seating arrangement was altered. The side aisles were removed and a wider centre aisle installed. This allowed for larger, more comfortable seats. The B&F Theatre chain took control of the theatre the same year.

In 1942 the theatre was purchased by Morris and Sam Rittenberg. They renovated it, employing the designer Jay English, and renamed the theatre Cinema Lumiere.

City of Toronto Archives, Series 1278, File 71

The Garden Theatre at 290 College Street as it appeared in the early decades of the twentieth century, when it possessed a roof garden. The covered roof over the garden space is evident in the photo. On the second floor there are two French balconies, adding to the elegance of the façade. There was no canopy over the entrance. The theatre was on the north side of College Street, a short distance west of Spadina Avenue.

In 1950, the Garden Billiard Academy opened on the second floor. In this year, next door, to the west of the theatre was the Melody Restaurant, at the rear of it the Frosty Ice Cream Company. Patrons were able to view a film and enjoy a coffee and sandwich after the movie and, in hot weather, purchase a cooling treat. In 1960 the billiard academy was renovated and renamed the New Garden Billiard Academy. By that year the eatery next door was called the Budapest Restaurant; the demographics of the neighbourhood were changing and the area was becoming more multicultural.

City of Toronto Archives, Series 1278, File 71

Undated photo showing the interior of the theatre after 1936. The side aisles have been removed, and a wider centre aisle added.

In 1967 the theatre closed and the site became the home of the Central Billiard Academy. The billiard academy closed in 1972, and during the years ahead the premises were leased for other commercial enterprises.

COLLEGE THEATRE

For several decades, the College Theatre's curved façade dominated the northwest corner of College Street and Dovercourt Road. Located at 960 College Street, it was another of the theatres constructed by the Allen brothers.

The College opened in 1921 under the ownership of Allen College Theatre Limited, but was leased to Famous Players Corporation. It was one of the largest theatres ever built on College Street west of Yonge, containing almost 1,500 seats, even though there was no balcony. The façade was exceedingly plain, with an unornamented cornice, similar to Allen's Parkdale and Allen's St. Clair Theatres. However, it was a comfortable

The College Theatre in 1947.

theatre, its auditorium possessing four aisles and plush seats. The sides of the auditorium were richly ornamented with Wedgewood-style designs, and on the ceiling there were similar motifs and Art Deco style chandeliers.

The theatre was immensely popular during the 1920s, but the years of the Great Depression were financially difficult as it was not easy to fill a theatre of its size. However, during the 1940s, it thrived as many of the factories supporting the war industries were located in the west end of the city, within easy travelling distance of the theatre.

On July 6, 1953, in the doorman's room there was a fire that was quickly extinguished by the manager. The audience was ordered to exit the theatre by the fire marshal, but 400 patrons refused to leave until emergency tickets were given out. Obviously they believed that there was no real danger or they would have departed the building quickly. They were correct, as the fire only inflicted $400 worth of damage.

During the 1960s, the theatre again experienced financial problems. The College experimented with various approaches to increase attendance. In November 1962 it held a Hockey Night, which was a

The auditorium of the College Theatre.

great success, but unfortunately that was the exception rather than the rule; the number of patrons continued to decline. The theatre closed on March 3, 1967, and was listed on the real estate market for $300,000. It was eventually purchased and the magnificent theatre demolished.

PLAYHOUSE THEATRE (MELODY)

As a teenager I was familiar with the College Street area north of the Kensington Market, but I do not remember the Playhouse Theatre. Located at 344 College Street, it was on the north side of the street, a few doors east of Brunswick Avenue. The theatre was on the ground-floor level of a three-storey building block, erected in the 1880s or 1890s.

Grouping two or more structures into a single building was an excellent business enterprise in the latter decades of the nineteenth century, as it was more economical to construct and maintain than detached structures. It also reduced the amount of land required. Landlords rented the

The Playhouse Theatre c. 1938, near Brunswick Avenue. Movies showing are Mae West in Klondike Annie *and Margaret Lindsay in* The Law in Her Hands, *both films released in 1936.*

first-floor levels for shops, and the floors above them for offices or residential apartments. The Playhouse rented space within such a building, occupying the equivalent of two stores. The theatre likely opened in the late-1920s or early 1930s.

The marquee stretched across the entire front, the large sign above the marquee attached to the façade between the second and third floors. At night, anyone living in the apartments on these floors was exposed to the bright lights of the sign. The box office was at the edge of the sidewalk, the entrance doors on either side.

I was unable to discover any information about the theatre in the archives. However, because it was on the ground floor, I am certain there would have been no balcony as the ceiling was not of sufficient height. The building extended back from College Street, so the auditorium would have been long and narrow, likely with a single aisle. In the decade when it opened, it would have most certainly possessed a small stage

143

for vaudeville acts. In the years ahead, the Playhouse was renamed the Melody Theatre.

There is a poster in the collection of the Toronto Reference Library, dated 1950, that advertises a live musical program at the Portuguese Melody Theatre at 344 College Street. The theatre was responding to the demographic changes in the neighbourhood and was screening Portuguese films. I was unable to discover the year that the theatre closed.

ODEON TORONTO (ODEON CARLTON)

I have included the Odeon Carlton Theatre in this book since, as I previously explained, I considered it one of my local theatres because in the 1950s I frequently travelled downtown to attend it. Whenever I entered its enormous lobby I was in awe of its elegant grandeur and viewed it as a true movie palace. However, unlike the movie palaces of yesteryear, such as the Imperial and Shea's Hippodrome, the Odeon was sleek and modern. Its architecture and interior trim reflected the finest trends of the second half of the twentieth century.

When the Odeon opened on September 9, 1948, the posters and ads advertised it as "The Showplace of the Dominion." As a teenager, I felt that this was no exaggeration, especially since it contained a restaurant on the mezzanine level. In that year, it was Canada's only restaurant inside a theatre. On frigid winter evenings, a friend and I often enjoyed fish and chips or Ritz Carlton "Red Hots" (hot dogs) in this eatery, managed by the Honey Dew Restaurants. The chain of eateries was famous for its orange drink that included "real pulp," as its advertisements stated. It was one of the most popular beverages at the CNE during this decade. The theatre had originally intended to offer a first-class restaurant on the premises but was unable to obtain a liquor licence.

As a teenager, I remember seeing the film star Dorothy Lamour on its stage in a live show that also featured the famous quartet The Four Lads, who were graduates of the St. Michael's Choir School on Bond Street in Toronto. Music from the enormous theatre organ on the right-hand side of the stage is another memory that remains with me. It was a magnificent instrument

The Odeon Toronto, later renamed the Odeon Carlton, on opening night, September 9, 1948. In the distance, the lights on the canopy of Maple Leaf Gardens are visible.

that surrounded the audience with rich sound, despite the cavernous size of the auditorium. Today, the organ resides at Queen's University in Kingston.

The theatre required two years and two and a half million dollars to build. It opened as the Odeon Toronto, the premier movie house in Toronto of the British Odeon chain. It contained 2,300 plush green-and-gold seats. The drapery and curtains surrounding the stage weighed two and a half tons, contoured to wrap around the front of the auditorium. Long horizontal lines, curved near the stage, swept the full length of the north and south walls. All floors were broadloom, possessing elegant floral designs with bright colours. The carpeting and colour scheme had been chosen by Eaton's College Street store, on the southwest corner of Yonge and College Streets. The trim throughout the theatre was blond-stained wood and stainless steel. The curved balcony swept across the width of the auditorium. At the rear of the theatre there was free parking for patrons from 6 p.m. onward. This information was obtained from the brochure provided to patrons on opening night.

Lobby and stairs to the mezzanine level, and the mural on the staircase depicting the various activities of the film industry.

For its inauguration, the theatre featured the North American premier of the J. Arthur Rank production of Dickens' classic tale *Oliver Twist*, with Alec Guinness as Fagan. Guinness was unable to attend on opening night, but Trevor Howard and Patricia Roc, both of whom were in the film, were present to add star status to the event. The seating was all reserved ticketing.

Later in the month, the naughty stars of the CNE Grandstand — Olsen and Johnson — attended the theatre. These stars had been warned by the Toronto morality squad to censor the jokes they told in their grandstand performances. Of course this edict drew greater crowds to their performances. A luncheon was held in their honour at the Carlton, but I doubt if they were served either fish and chips or hotdogs in the restaurant.

In January 1949, the film *Scott of the Antarctic* was screened at the Carlton, starring John Mills. No luncheon was held for this show, although frozen fish sticks would have been appropriate.

Ontario Archives, RG56-11-0-305-3

View from the stage of the auditorium of the Odeon Carlton.

By the early 1970s, it became obvious that the Carlton was too large to operate profitably. For a brief period, the city considered purchasing it as a home for the Canadian Opera Company. However, this was deemed financially ruinous, as the city was already subsidizing the O'Keefe Centre, now named the Sony Centre for the Performing Arts.

The Odeon Carlton shut its doors in September 1975 and was later demolished. A modern office building is on the site today, and on its ground floor is a multiplex theatre named the Carlton Cinemas.

CHAPTER NINE

Theatres on Bloor Street West

MADISON (MIDTOWN, CAPRI, EDEN, BLOOR HOT DOCS CINEMA)

When I was a teenager in the 1950s, for two summers I was employed at the Dominion Bank (now the TD) on the southeast corner of Bloor West and Bathurst Streets. The bank's largest customer was a relatively unknown merchant named Ed Mirvish, who had converted two old houses on the southeast corner of Bloor and Markham Streets into shops. Mirvish eventually took over the entire block, creating the famous Honest Ed's bargain store. One of his slogans was, "Often imitated but never duplicated." I find it sad that this Toronto landmark will disappear on December 31, 2016.

Part of my job was to deliver bank drafts to the shops between Bathurst Street and Ossington Avenue. I often strolled past the Midtown Theatre at 506 Bloor West. During these years it was screening mostly horror flicks. I was fascinated by the colourful posters outside the theatre and often gazed up longingly at the movies listed on the marquee. However, because the theatre's location was distant from my home, I was never inside it.

In the early twentieth century the Bathurst/Bloor district was serviced by two major streetcar lines. At the time, builders were not required to provide laneways between houses to accommodate automobiles. Thus, the

*The Midtown Theatre
c. 1945.*

City of Toronto Archives, Series 1278, File 103

homes in the area were constructed close together, increasing the population density. This is true of much of Toronto's downtown. In later decades, when automobile ownership became more common, space was taken from the rear gardens of the houses to construct laneways behind the houses, parallel to the streets. The lanes, flanked by garages, remain today.

During the 1940s and 1950s, the city's children used these laneways as playgrounds, which were superior to anything that modern designers could ever create. They were private worlds, away from the prying eyes of adults, where kids explored and learned about life, sometimes even about sex. The veracity of the sex lessons was often doubtful, but the laneways did teach kids how to "exaggerate." Another source of exaggerated sexual activity was the back rows of theatres, although by today's standards they were relatively innocent.

Because the streets around Bathurst and Bloor saw a lot of pedestrian traffic, it was an ideal location for a theatre. The site chosen for the Madison was on the north side of Bloor, between Bathurst and Albany Avenue (named Lippincott on the south side of Bloor). When the Madison opened on December 23, 1913, it was one of Toronto's earliest "picture palace" theatres. It possessed just over 700 plush leather seats, including the balcony and ground-floor level.

In 1913 silent films were becoming the latest entertainment craze. Until Allen's Bloor Theatre (Lee's Palace) opened in 1919 and the Alhambra in 1920, the Madison was the main theatre on Bloor Street, near Bathurst. It remained a popular local theatre for several decades. In 1940, Twentieth-Century Theatres took over the property. They demolished the building, except for the two side walls. The architectural firm of Kaplan and Sprachman designed the new theatre, which opened in May 1941 — renamed the Midtown.

During the 1950s, attendance at the Midtown slowly dwindled. To attract patrons, it screened mostly horror films. The theatre remained under the management of Famous Players until 1967, but at some time during this period its name was changed to the Capri.

In 1973, it was again renamed, becoming the Eden, screening censored adult films containing scenes that today are often shown on regular TV programs during prime-time hours. Times have indeed changed. The adult flicks at the Eden ended in 1979 and the name was changed to the Bloor Theatre. The theatre returned to screening family-type films.

From 1980 to 1999 the theatre was managed by Carm Bordonaro and his partners, as part of the Festival Cinema Chain. Finally, the Bordonaro family purchased the theatre to ensure that it would remain an active movie house.

In 2011 the Blue Ice Group invested in the property. The theatre was renovated and reopened on November 4th of the same year, renamed the Bloor Hot Docs Cinema. Its interior is luxurious, though not in the same manner as the movie palaces of the early decades of the twentieth century, as the Hot Docs Cinema's design is modern.

It remains one of the most comfortable and attractive theatres in Toronto, specializing in documentary films that audiences otherwise

Interior of the Bloor Hot Docs Theatre, 2014.

might not have a chance to view. I sincerely hope that Toronto never loses this exceptional theatre venue.

ALLEN'S BLOOR THEATRE
(BLOOR THEATRE, LEE'S PALACE)

On a summer afternoon in 2014, I journeyed to the intersection of Bloor and Bathurst Streets in search of one of Toronto's old movie houses. I had never attended the theatre and did not remember it from when I worked in the area in the 1950s. However, I had read about the Allen brothers, Jule and Jay, who built the theatre.

As previously mentioned, the exteriors of the Allens' theatres were often relatively plain, but the interiors were richly ornamented, the exuberant plaster ornamentations and gold-painted trim portraying hints of the cathedrals and palaces of Europe.

The former Allen's Bloor Theatre located at 529 Bloor Street West. The façade of the building now has colourful graffiti art. Photo was taken in 2014.

When I finally arrived at the location of the former Allen's Bloor Theatre, at 529 Bloor Street West, few traces remained of the luxurious theatre that had been on the site. Now named Lee's Palace, it is a nightclub and live music venue. Its façade is covered with colourful graffiti art created by Al Runt, one of the city's most accomplished graffiti artists.

The Allen's Bloor Theatre opened on March 10, 1919, with the silent film *Don't Change Your Husband*, starring Gloria Swanson. It was one of a series of three films with a similar theme, all starring Gloria Swanson.

The theatre was in direct competition with the Madison that had opened in 1913 further west along the street. Allen's Bloor was the smallest of the Allen theatres, with about 700 seats, as opposed to their other venues that boasted 1,200 to 1,500 seats.

The marquee of Allen's Bloor was small, with three windows above it, topped with Roman arches. Windows of similar design were on opposite sides of them. These small touches, along with the dentils in the cornice, gave the façade a classic look. The architect of Allen's Bloor was C. Howard Crane of Detroit, who designed all the Allen venues. As usual, its auditorium contained a stage for vaudeville and an orchestra pit for the musicians. Over the stage area was an enormous archway, with decorative plaster ornamentations surrounding it. The vaulted ceiling resembled a great cathedral.

The theatre was highly successful, but unfortunately the Allen brothers overextended their finances. In 1923 the chain was purchased by Famous Players, who renamed Allen's Bloor to the Bloor Theatre.

The Bloor remained an active theatre until February 16, 1957, still operated by Famous Players. After it closed, the premises were renovated for other purposes. It was the Blue Orchid Restaurant for a few years and also a bank. In 1985 it became Lee's Palace.

DORIC THEATRE (LA SCALA)

The Doric Theatre at 1094 Bloor Street West was located near Gladstone Avenue, on the north side of Bloor, a short distance east of Dufferin Street. Plans for the theatre were submitted to the city in November 1914, when the address was 1108 Bloor West. The postal numbers were later revised.

The building containing the Doric was unusual, as it was only one storey in height. It was a small venue, possessing only 527 seats and no balcony, truly a neighbourhood theatre, dependant on the patrons who lived within walking distance. The theatre was renovated several times throughout the decades. When it originally opened, the façade was neo-classical in design, with two Ionic columns supporting a portico. It is rather odd that a theatre containing Ionic columns was named the Doric. Beneath the portico, recessed from the sidewalk, were the entrance doors.

The façade of the theatre was renovated by Kaplan and Sprachman in 1934. A new canopy was installed to contain the marquee, which was typical of many Toronto theatres during that decade, although there was no large sign attached to the façade to advertise the theatre's name. However, bold letters on either side at the top of the canopy displayed the word *Doric*, the signs clearly visible at night when the marquee was ablaze with light.

The Doric Theatre. This photo was taken during a gas seepage on January 18, 1941, when Sam Lester was the manager.

The box office was in the centre of the entranceway, the theatre's doors located only three or four feet from the sidewalk. On either side of the doors were display spaces showing the films being screened and advertisements for future attractions.

Throughout its life, the Doric Theatre remained a single-storey building. There were never any residential apartments above it to generate income to offset the expenses of the theatre. Also, because the building was quite small and squeezed between other structures, there was no space for rental shops either. Thus, the sole income of the theatre was derived from ticket sales. This was acceptable as long as the movie house was well attended, but during the lean days of the 1950s the theatre fell on harsh times. For a brief period it screened Italian films and was named La Scala.

The Doric closed its doors in 1955, one of the first theatres to succumb to the decrease in attendance created by the increasing popularity of television. Today, there is a Tim Hortons on the site.

ALHAMBRA THEATRE (BARONET, EVE)

The Alhambra Theatre at 568 Bloor Street West, a few doors west of Bathurst Street, was another theatre that was a familiar sight when I was a teenager. Every morning when I alighted from the Bloor streetcar on my way to work, the first thing that caught my eye was the imposing Alhambra Theatre, located near the intersection. The bank where I worked is now a takeout pizza restaurant, but at least the building survives. Unfortunately, the Alhambra was demolished.

The feature of the Alhambra that I remember the most was the magnificent marquee, which swept across the front, advertising the two daily features. In the 1950s the theatre was no longer screening the latest Hollywood hits, but it remained competitive with the other theatres in the area. It showed films daily from 2 p.m. until near midnight.

The Alhambra Theatre c. 1930, the sign on the west wall referring to the films as "photo plays."

City of Toronto Archives, Series 1278, File 14

There were often long lines at its box office, particularly on Friday and Saturday evenings.

The Alhambra commenced life as a vaudeville and silent movie house. Its façade contained Moorish architectural detailing, from which its name was derived. The original 1920s marquee was rectangular and flattened again the building, which was the equivalent of four storeys in height. This allowed its ceiling to be sufficiently high to accommodate a balcony that wrapped around three sides of the auditorium.

The Alhambra's inaugural show in 1920 was at 2 p.m., featuring the film *Back Stage* with Fatty Arbuckle. Films in the early 1920s were often only an hour in length, so they were supplemented with live stage performances. At the opening of the theatre a short play, *The Woman Thou Gavest Me*, based on a book by Hall Caine, was performed. The evening performance at 7 p.m. offered the same program. It ended with a rousing rendition of "God Save the King," which was the usual manner in which theatre performances ended in this decade. This tradition lasted until

Ontario Archives, RG 56-11-0-267

Auditorium of the Alhambra c. 1950.

the end of the 1940s. I remember it well, and also recall that some people exited the theatre while it was playing.

During the years ahead the theatre remained profitable. Several improvements were initiated, including adding a candy bar in 1946. In 1949 the original marquee was replaced, as well as the seating. When movie attendance declined in the late 1960s, in an effort to keep the theatre open, the Alhambra screened older films because they were less expensive to rent. Around this time the theatre was renamed the Baronet, a rather classy name for a venue that had become somewhat tattered and worn. Despite its noble name, the theatre doors were finally permanently closed.

Sadly, the theatre was demolished in 1985. In the building erected on the site, there was a Swiss Chalet restaurant on the first level. I visited it on several occasions, and as I enjoyed the barbeque chicken, for a few moments my thoughts would drift back to the 1950s, when the Alhambra Theatre was in its prime. This restaurant has also disappeared.

ESQUIRE THEATRE (LYNDHURST)

The Esquire Theatre was a small neighbourhood theatre built for Mr. R. Luxton. Located on the north side of Bloor Street West, it was a few doors east of Durie Street. When the theatre opened in 1926 it was named the Lyndhurst. The name was changed to the Esquire about the year 1937. The architects were Kaplan and Sprachman, who designed the theatre in the Art Deco style. The façade facing Bloor Street was symmetrical, with little architectural ornamentation, the cornice containing simple brick patterns. The box office was originally inside the lobby, but was later relocated to the edge of the sidewalk, as seen in the 1937 photo. On the second floor were residential apartments, three of the windows of the apartments having stone trim above them.

The Lyndhurst Theatre contained about five hundred seats, with leather bottoms and mohair backs. When it opened, it was considered quite luxurious and attracted many patrons from the surrounding Jane/Bloor West area. It did not have a balcony. In 1950 the back two rows of seats were removed to allow a candy bar to be installed.

The Esquire Theatre at 2290 Bloor Street West, c. 1937.

I chatted with a cousin of mine who remembers attending Saturday afternoon matinees at the Esquire regularly in the early 1950s. In that decade, his family lived in Malton and there was no local theatre that was convenient to attend. However, West York Coach Lines maintained regular service between Malton and the intersection of Bloor and Jane Streets. Once a week, my cousin and his friends hopped on the bus and travelled to the city to go to the Esquire. The Bowery Boys films were among their favourite attractions.

I received a report from a person who attended the theatre sometime between 1951 and when it closed. During those years he lived near Runnymede and Bloor. He said, "The theatre was not in good condition at this time and was not especially pleasing to visit." The two films he saw there were *Knock on Any Door* (released in 1949) and *Ruby Gentry* (released in 1952).

The theatre closed in 1955 and was renovated for other commercial enterprises.

KENWOOD THEATRE

Unfortunately, the 1936 photo of a men's race on Bloor Street is the only one I was able to discover of the Kenwood Theatre in the Toronto Archives. A *Globe and Mail* reporter snapped a picture of the marathon race and the theatre is visible in the background. The theatre was located at 962 Bloor Street West, on the north side of the street, a short distance east of Dovercourt Road.

Toronto Archives, Series 1278, File 91, *Globe and Mail*, G&M 29609

This photo, depicting a marathon run on Bloor Street on April 14, 1936, provides a poor view of the Kenwood Theatre, but was the only picture in the archives that included it.

Similar to the Grover Theatre on the Danforth, the Kenwood received its name from the area's telephone exchange. Kenwood telephone numbers were introduced to 4,900 customers in 1920, the eleventh exchange that the city created; it centred on the Bloor West and Dufferin area. At that time it was possible to identify where in Toronto people lived by their telephone exchange. For example, everyone knew that the exchange Empire was a downtown number.

Plans for the theatre were submitted to the city by Kaplan and Sprachman in May 1929, and the Kenwood opened in 1930. The façade reflected the Art Deco style and possessed a large overhanging cornice. There was a small shop on the west side of the theatre's entrance that was a part of the building and was rented to various tenants. On the second floor there were residential apartments. The Kenwood contained almost 600 upholstered seats, installed by the Globe Furniture Company of Waterloo. This firm supplied the hand-carved woodwork for the Metropolitan United Church at Queen East and Church Street when it was rebuilt following a disastrous fire in June 1928. The quality of the company's workmanship can be admired today, especially in the chancel.

The auditorium of the Kenwood had a concrete floor and there was no balcony. On the ground floor, there was a central aisle only. The box office was at the edge of the sidewalk. The foyer was only twenty-four feet wide, as the building was long and narrow, extending a considerable distance back from the street. The theatre was renovated just three years after it opened, by the firm of Kaplan and Sprachman.

During the early forties the theatre was managed by Al Perly, the future father-in-law of Bob Rae, former MP and premier of Ontario.

In 1946 the theatre was again renovated, and standing room was created in an area that had previously been a part of the lobby. In this year, the theatre's owner was Nat Taylor, who in the years ahead owned Loew's Uptown and went into partnership with Garth Drabinsky to form Odeon Cineplex Corporation.

In 1947, a candy bar was added.

In July 1951 the manager of the Kenwood was Grant Millar. He gave a family that had been evicted from their home in the district free passes to the theatre for an entire year, as well as free bags of candies for the children.

He became known as the "good Samaritan manager." In this year, the theatre was under the management of the Twentieth-Century chain.

The theatre closed in 1957, but remained listed on the real estate market in 1959. It was eventually sold and became a store named Krainska Knyha, which sold Ukrainian products such as clothing and table linens.

PARADISE THEATRE (EVE'S PARADISE)

During the summer of 2014, in my quest to locate and photograph Toronto's old local theatres, none of the discoveries surprised and pleased me more than the sight of the Paradise Theatre. Located at 1008 Bloor Street West, it is on the northwest corner of Bloor and Westmoreland Avenue. However, I must admit that my pleasure slowly became tinged with a hint of sadness, as its impressive marquee was blank, devoid of the names of films, and the spaces where posters had once advertised films were empty or contained faded posters. One of the spaces had graffiti defacing it. The theatre was akin to a grand old lady whose glory days had vanished and was now a relic from the past.

Despite this, I must confess I was gladdened by the realization that at least the theatre had survived, and despite the passing of the many decades, its façade of glazed bricks still sparkled in the afternoon sun. Its marquee may have been empty, but it was well preserved and as attractive as when it was first installed. In my opinion, the Paradise is an architectural gem.

The site where it exists has a long history in the story of Toronto's local theatres. The first theatre built on this site was named the Kitchener. It opened its doors to screen silent movies in 1909, in the days prior to the First World War. The cost of constructing the theatre was $3,000. To build the Paradise, the old Kitchener Theatre was gutted, very little of it being retained.

The present-day cinema opened in 1937, designed by the Lithuanian-born Benjamin Brown, one of the city's famous architects. He had previously created the Reading Building in 1925, the Tower Building in 1927, and the Balfour Building in 1930, all located on Spadina Avenue. Brown also was the architect of the infamous Victory Theatre.

Toronto Archives, Series 1278, File 10

Paradise Theatre c. 1946.

Benjamin Brown chose the Art Deco style for the Paradise Theatre. The tall rectangular windows on the second floor and the narrow rows of raised bricks create the impression of extra height. Its cornice is relatively unadorned, with a raised centre section in the central position, typical of many Art Deco buildings. When it opened in 1937, the auditorium contained a small stage, with dressing rooms to accommodate actors when live performances were offered. It was an intimate theatre, containing a small lobby and less than 500 seats, including the balcony.

The theatre changed ownership several times during the decades ahead, but, except for a period in the 1980s when it screened soft porno and was named Eve's Paradise, it always retained its original name. Italian films were screened in the 1960s. In the 1990s, it was a repertory theatre, part of the Festival chain.

By the early years of the twenty-first century, the Paradise had become somewhat shabby, its projectors having insufficient power to properly illuminate the film-prints, and the sound system was in poor shape. It closed in 2006, but in 2007 was listed as a heritage property. Unfortunately, because the laws are very lax, this did not ensure that it would not be demolished.

However, this story has a happy ending. The Paradise Theatre was purchased by Moray Tawse, who plans to restore it to its original glory. The plan is to turn it into an arts centre and community theatre, a valuable addition to Toronto's cultural scene.

ODEON HUMBER (HUMBER CINEMAS)

Designed by Jay Isadore English, at a cost of $400,000, the Odeon Humber Theatre opened on January 27, 1948. The Odeon Humber was a large theatre, containing 1,200 seats. It was constructed by the British Odeon Chain, a subsidiary of the Rank Organisation.

My first visit to the Humber was in 1954, the year that Hurricane Hazel devastated the city, causing destruction and loss of life when the Humber and Don Rivers flooded their banks.

The Odeon Humber Theatre was divided into two auditoriums in 1975. One theatre was on the ground-floor level and the other was in the space that had previously been the balcony. It received a $400,000 renovation in 1999, when larger seats, digital sound, and a new concession stand were installed. The theatre was eventually bought by the Cineplex Odeon Corporation, but the company closed it in 2003. The building was empty for several years and was in danger of being

The Odeon Humber Theatre in 1949.

The impressive auditorium of the Odeon Humber in 1948.

demolished for condominiums. However, it was rescued by Rui Pereira, owner of the Kingsway Cinema, who reopened it as a multiplex theatre named the Humber Cinemas, with five auditoriums. The theatre space in the balcony remained intact, but the ground floor contained four small theatres.

I hope that the Humber Cinemas survives in the years ahead, as it is representative of the local theatres that at one time were in almost every community across the city.

UNIVERSITY THEATRE

Located at 100 Bloor Street West, the University Theatre was a short distance west of Bay Street. One of Toronto's most popular theatres for almost four decades, it was not a local theatre, as it attracted patrons from across the entire city. However, as with the Odeon Carlton, I have included it among the theatres in this book as I attended it as frequently as the theatres closer to my home.

In many respects, the University was a modern "movie palace," even though the experts declared it too intimate to be classified as such. I do not agree with this reasoning. After all, including the auditorium and the balcony, it contained 1,350 seats, manufactured by Canadian Theatre Chair Company. Its luxurious lobby was the equivalent of two storeys in height, with a grand staircase connecting the lower and mezzanine levels. Its wide screen was one of the largest ever installed in the city, ideal for widescreen megahits.

Admittedly, Loew's Downtown (the Elgin) was larger, with 1,900 seats, but I believe that the University was truly a movie palace in both size and design. Its sleek modern façade had a dazzling Art Moderne-style marquee and towering signage; at its pinnacle were the words "Famous Players." The auditorium possessed modernistic vertical lines, emphasizing its vast height. It was one of the greatest postwar theatres ever built in Canada and was Famous Players' attempt to compete with the Odeon Carlton. The University opened on March 25, 1949, with the film *Joan of Arc*, starring Ingrid Bergman.

City of Toronto Archives, Series 1278, File 162

The University Theatre in 1949, when the opening-night film was still screening.

My memories of the University Theatre are associated with some of the greatest megahits of the latter half of the twentieth century. Seeing these films usually required that a ticket be purchased in advance. Tickets displayed the seat and row number, similar to live performances at the Royal Alexandra Theatre. There were intermissions halfway through the films. This feature, along with the ticketing system, added to the sense of occasion when one was attending screenings.

One of the first films that I recall seeing at the University was in 1956, *The Ten Commandments*. In 1957, the University was the first Toronto theatre to offer Cinerama, the wide-screen format, which was an instant hit. Other ticketed films that I remember are *Ben Hur* (1959), *Cleopatra* (1963), *My Fair Lady* (1964), *Doctor Zhivago* (1965), and *The Agony and the Ecstasy* (1965).

The last megahit that I associate with the University is *Apocalypse Now* (1979). This Vietnam War film was not reserved-ticket seating. However, I can still recall how the entire theatre vibrated in the scene where the military helicopters roared across the beach, guns blazing, while the majestic "Ride of the Valkyries" from Wagner's famous opera *Die Walküre* thundered from the theatre's Dolby sound system. It is no wonder that the film played at the theatre for fifty-two weeks.

Due to its enormous size, the theatre eventually developed financial problems when attendance declined. In the mid-1980s, the theatre's manager was quoted as saying that even if the theatre were able to screen another hit with the same potential ticket sales as *Apocalypse Now*, the venue would not be profitable.

The University shut its doors in 1986. The building was demolished, except for its façade, which today is the entrance to a retail store. However, the theatre's box office remains, facing Bloor Street. Every time I pass it, I remember the great films that I saw at this venerable theatre.

View of the University Theatre's auditorium, taken near the stage.

Ontario Archives, RG 56-11-0-323-10

CHAPTER TEN

Theatres on St. Clair Avenue West

OAKWOOD THEATRE

The Oakwood is one of Toronto's old movie theatres that I remember well. As a young boy in the 1940s, I caught my first glimpse of it from the windows of an Oakwood streetcar, when our family journeyed downtown. In that decade it was illegal to screen movies on Sundays, but if it were a hot day we passed the shuttered theatre when we went to Centre Island.

When I was older, I boarded the streetcars to go to the Oakwood Theatre to view films. I do not recall any of the films that I saw, but I remember that I was impressed by the size and grandeur of its auditorium. It was huge compared with the two theatres within walking distance of our house — the Grant and the Colony. As well, the Oakwood's candy bar was larger. The theatre always screened two films, and between films, patrons who wished to enjoy a cigarette went out on the street to smoke. A friend and I sometimes mingled with the smokers and strolled in without purchasing a ticket. We considered this a "real lark," as we used to say.

The Oakwood Theatre was located at 165 Oakwood Avenue, in the city's historic District of Earlscourt, which centred on St. Clair Avenue West and Dufferin Street. In the first decade of the twentieth century, the area was not part of the City of Toronto, as it was remote from the downtown area. The enormous hill north of Davenport Road created a

City of Toronto Archives, Series 1278, File 116

The Oakwood Theatre when it was screening Dark Victory, *starring Bette Davis, Humphrey Bogart, and George Brent, released in January 1939.*

geographic barrier that separated it from the city below the hill. If residents of Earlscourt wished to travel to downtown Toronto, they walked down the hill and boarded a streetcar at Van Horne (now named Dupont) and Dufferin Streets. The return journey up the hill was considerably more arduous, especially in winter.

The first streetcar line that travelled up over the hill was built on Yonge Street in the 1890s. Within a few years, another streetcar line was constructed on Avenue Road. However, in the Earlscourt area, the isolation did not end until 1913, when a streetcar line was built along St. Clair Avenue West that connected with the Avenue Road streetcar. The St. Clair streetcar extended from Avenue Road as far west as Lansdowne Avenue.

After the streetcar line was opened, commercial development along St. Clair Avenue West rapidly expanded. As a result, more houses appeared on the streets to the north and south of St. Clair Avenue. However, it remained a daunting journey to travel downtown on the streetcar. Most people only journeyed to the city's core for work, visiting relatives, or an occasional shopping excursion.

However, because the population of the Earlscourt area had increased, the potential for local movie houses within walking distance of the homes was readily seen. One of the busier north-south streets in the area was Oakwood Avenue. Thus, the intersection at Oakwood and St. Clair was viewed as an ideal location for a theatre.

A real estate developer, James Crang Jr., purchased property on the east side of Oakwood, a short distance north of St. Clair. The theatre opened in 1917, its postal address 165 Oakwood Avenue. Its only competition at the time was the Royal George Theatre, which was considerably smaller. The façade of the Oakwood Theatre was relatively unadorned, the slanted roof above the façade possessing terracotta tiles, considered quite fashionable in the early decades of the twentieth century. Below the marquee, at either end, were large rounded glass pillar-like structures. The box office was in a central position between them, the doors to the theatre recessed behind the box office.

The theatre's auditorium contained almost 1,400 wood-back seats. The seating was arranged with a centre section and aisles on either side of it. There were two side sections, but no balcony. The ceiling contained horizontal decorative lines, similar to the theatre's façade. The north and south walls possessed a combination of horizontal and vertical lines, the design simple but attractive. On the ceiling were large crystal chandeliers, though I attended the theatre in the late 1940s and throughout the 1950s and do not recall ever having seen them. They might have been removed due to maintenance costs, or perhaps the reason I do not remember them is because I usually entered the theatre after the houselights had been dimmed, as the movie was already in progress.

In the 1950s, people departed their homes to attend a movie at whatever time suited them. They were not concerned about the starting times of the films. After viewing a movie, they remained seated to view the part that they had missed. This meant that people were entering and departing throughout the screenings. Ushers and usherettes were required, using flashlights to assist people to find their seats in the dark. This is not as necessary today, as patrons tend to arrive at the beginning of a film and when they enter a theatre the lights are on.

One of my cousins worked at the Oakwood Theatre in the 1950s as an usherette. We all envied her as we knew that while showing people to their seats, she was able to catch a glimpse of the movies. On evenings when there were few patrons, she could stand at the back of the theatre and watch the movies. When I attended the Oakwood Theatre, it always screened two films. Due to a tight budget, it was unable to afford to rent recently released films.

The Oakwood shut its doors in 1962 and was demolished. On the site today is an apartment building with the address 161 Oakwood Avenue.

CHRISTIE THEATRE

The Christie Theatre, located at 665 St. Clair Avenue West, was on the south side of the street, between Wychwood Avenue and Christie Street. I was unable to discover much information on this theatre, but according to the website of the Earlscourt History Club, the theatre opened in 1919.

The Christie was operated by the B&F chain. In 1923, according to an article in the files of the Toronto Archives, the Christie Theatre became the first theatre to screen double-bill features of films that were not recent releases. This was an important innovation that was instantly copied by other neighbourhood theatres, allowing them to compete with the larger downtown venues that featured the latest Hollywood movies. Viewing two films for the price of one soon became popular with audiences throughout the city.

The theatre was taken over by Famous Players and renovated by the architects Kaplan and Sprachman in 1936. Over the years the number of seats in the theatre had varied, but in 1936 there were 877.

I remember the theatre well, because as a teenager I visited the Strathcona Roller Skating Rink on Christie Street, a short distance south of St. Clair Avenue. On these occasions, following an hour or two at the rink I sometimes attended the Christie Theatre.

In 1963 the owners of the building where the Christie Theatre was located demanded a 50 percent rent increase. Rennie Fode, who had been managing the theatre since 1961, had originally put down a $1,500

City of Toronto Archives Series 1278, File 44

Many of Toronto's old theatres are basically not documented, and for some the photos are of poor quality. The Christie, on the right-hand side of the picture, is one of them. The photo, taken on September 28, 1928, shows repairs being made to the streetcar tracks on St. Clair Avenue. The view is to the east.

investment. The increase in rent meant that it was impossible for him to continue operating. In June of 1963, the Christie closed and the premises were converted into a dance club, The Maple Leaf Ballroom. U2 played there in February 1981. The building remains on St. Clair Avenue in 2016, but is a thrift store.

ST. CLAIR THEATRE

I caught my first glimpse of the St. Clair Theatre in the early 1940s, as a young boy accompanying my mother when she went shopping on St. Clair. I enjoyed the trips as we usually passed Harry Bell's Shoe Store, where there was a huge German Shepherd that reclined at the entrance of the shop. The dog was featured on the cover of the scribblers given

City of Toronto Archives, Salmon Collection, Series 1278, File 151

Gazing toward the northeast corner of Dufferin and St. Clair, in March 1920, the marquee of the Allen's St. Clair Theatre is visible in the distance.

to children who visited the store. On the back cover were copies of the multiplication tables. If Mr. Bell came outside the store, he always gave me a scribbler.

After my father immigrated to Toronto in 1921, St. Clair Theatre was a favourite hangout for him and his six brothers, since they were living nearby on Earlscourt Avenue. On warm evenings they often cruised along St. Clair, attempting to catch the eye of a pretty young woman. If my dad were successful, he invited the gal to attend the St. Clair Theatre. During the show, somehow his arm found its way around her shoulder. Perhaps my grandmother overheard my father's stories about the theatre and this was one of the reasons she objected to movie theatres, fearing that they promoted promiscuous behaviour.

In 1948 my family began attending a church located near Dufferin and St. Clair, and I strolled past the theatre on my way to Sunday school. On these occasions I remembered the stories I had overheard my father telling about his youthful indiscretions and longed to be old enough to perform a few of my own. Alas, I was forced to be content with the Sunday school teacher's version of Samson and Delilah. I was certain that a film version of this tale would be much more risqué. Unfortunately, when the movie *Samson and Delilah* was released in January 1949, it was an "adult" film and I was too young to purchase a ticket. In 1953 I saw the film *Salome*, starring Rita Hayworth, and my suspicions about Bible stories were confirmed.

The St. Clair Theatre was built by the Allen brothers in 1921. They already owned Allen's Danforth, Allen Theatre (Tivoli) at Adelaide and Victoria, Allen's Bloor (Lee's Palace), and Allen's Parkdale (the Parkdale). The architect of the St. Clair was C. Howard Crane, at the time employed by the firm of Hynes, Feldman and Watson. The St. Clair's yellow-brick façades on the south and east were unadorned, except for decorative stone detailing below the cornices. However, similar to those of other Allen theatres, the interior was tastefully extravagant, especially the high ceiling with its ornamental plaster trim and classical detailing. The theatre faithfully displayed the luxury that Allen patrons expected.

However, in the 1920s the theatre possessed no air conditioning, which was uncomfortable during Toronto's hot summers. When my father said that he had "hot times" in the back rows of the St. Clair Theatre, perhaps I misunderstood what he meant.

The St. Clair has the distinction of being the only theatre in the world visited by my grandmother. She saw the movie *Captains Courageous* there in 1937. She lived to be ninety-six years old and never again darkened the doors of a theatre. Perhaps my grandfather should have sat with her in the back row and cuddled her during the suspenseful parts of the film. On the other hand, she might have considered this to be "promiscuous behaviour."

The theatre was extensively renovated in 1950, when new seats were installed. The St. Clair was one of the few theatres that had a candy bar as well as a candy machine in the lobby. The machine was operated by inserting 6 cents (the penny placed on top of the nickel). If this was not done in this exact manner, the machine failed to operate.

The popularity of the St. Clair Theatre remained throughout the 1950s, but when attendance dwindled in the 1960s, the theatre was no longer profitable. The wonderful auditorium the Allen brothers had

Auditorium of the Allen's St. Clair Theatre.

created was divided into two screening spaces. For a few years, Italian films were shown, but this venture also eventually ended.

The property along St. Clair had greatly increased in value, and developers were anxious to purchase the building. It was sold and the space divided into shops. Fortunately, the building survives to this day, though few would ever guess that it was once a highly popular movie house.

MAJOR ST. CLAIR THEATRE (CINEMA ITALIA)

When the Major St. Clair Theatre at 1780 St. Clair Avenue West opened in 1924, it was located in a working-class district, remote from the downtown. Situated a short distance east of Old Weston Road, the theatre was originally part of the Allen chain. Because it was easily accessible on the St. Clair and Weston Road streetcar lines, it remained a popular local theatre for several decades. The theatre contained 599 leatherette seats, separated by two aisles, and no balcony.

A letter dated September 1940 tells of a complaint by a woman who stated that she witnessed children and young teenagers watching *You Can't Fool Your Wife* at the Major St. Clair. The woman claimed the movie "exalted the importance of a woman to make herself beautiful at all times, which was less pernicious than the positive teaching that a man cannot get advancement in the business world unless he is loose morally." Because she contacted the censors, they reviewed the film again and removed more of the dialogue. They also told the woman, "How this picture slipped past the censors is a mystery." The film was a light comedy, but in the 1940s what was considered acceptable differed greatly from that of today.

When attendance at the theatre dwindled, the Major St. Clair was renamed Cinema Italia and screened Italian movies. Eventually the building was sold to a church community and remains today as a place of worship.

Ontario Archives, RG 56-11-0-280-1

This photo of the Major St. Clair was likely taken about 1945, as the film Man from Down Under, *starring Charles Laughton, was released in 1943.*

Interior of the Major St. Clair in November 1970.

Ontario Archives, RG 56-11-0-280

RADIO CITY THEATRE

The Radio City Theatre was built in 1936 for R.R. Dennis, its architect the well-known Jay English. The theatre was located adjacent to the southern loop of the Vaughan bus and the northern terminus of the Bathurst streetcars. The theatre's address was 1454 Bathurst Street, a short distance south of St. Clair Avenue West. Its auditorium contained about 800 seats. The lobby was richly carpeted and included a fireplace. There was no balcony.

The first time I visited the Radio City Theatre, I was too young to attend unaccompanied. As a result, my parents allowed an adult neighbour to take a friend, my brother, and me to see Walt Disney's animated film *Snow White and the Seven Dwarfs*. The film had been released in 1937, but I saw it at the Radio City in 1943.

As a child, I thought the theatre was amazing. Its size and grandeur appeared palatial, worthy of the Prince Charming that rescued Snow White.

I did not attend the theatre again until I was of sufficient age to ride the Vaughan bus on my own. However, I rarely went there, since by that

Ontario Archives, RG 56-11-0-313-1

Radio City Theatre c. 1941.

Ontario Archives, RG 56-11-0-313

Auditorium of the Radio City.

time the larger and more attractive Vaughan Theatre had opened nearby. Both theatres were managed by the B&F chain.

During a screening of an Italian movie released in 1947, *Genoveffa di Brabante*, the lineups at the box office of the Radio City were so lengthy that the crowds became unruly. A policeman was hired to maintain order. The film, a tale of adventure and chivalry during the Crusades, was held over for several weeks.

The theatre's doors shut permanently in 1975 and the building was soon demolished. The site today contains a low-rise building that is employed for other commercial purposes.

VAUGHAN THEATRE

As previously mentioned, the Grant and Colony Theatres were my local theatres in the days when my parents allowed me to attend only theatres within walking distance of our house on Lauder Avenue. However, when I was ten years old, my parents purchased a newspaper delivery route for me. I delivered the *Toronto Star* to over sixty customers on our street. Papers sold for 3 cents, and in my eyes, the profits from my business enterprise were immense.

Children's bus fares were 3 cents cash or ten tickets for 25 cents. Having attained great affluence, I pleaded with my parents for permission to travel to the theatres on St. Clair Avenue West. The St. Clair Theatre I was able to walk to, but the Vaughan was too far away. With my money and parents' permission, my first goal was to attend the Vaughan Theatre, a few doors west of the intersection of St. Clair and Vaughan Road.

Because I had newspapers to deliver, it was important that I return home by 5 p.m. However, I must admit that after attending a matinee at the Vaughan, my customers sometimes waited longer than usual for their papers. I never explained to them why I was late. Visiting the Vaughan was worth the risk of losing a customer.

The feature of the theatre that I remember the most was the air conditioning. The theatre had opened in 1947, and everything was modern and up-to-date. The refreshing temperatures it maintained were a welcomed

Ontario Archives, 56-11-0-324-1

*The Vaughan
Theatre in 1947.*

treat after travelling on the hot Vaughan bus. I felt the cool air against my face the instant I opened one of the modern glass doors that spread across the entrance of the theatre. As we liked to say as kids, it was "Popsicle cool." In the 1940s, air conditioning was only available at Eaton's, Simpsons, theatres, and a few wealthy homes in Forest Hill or Rosedale.

Plans for the theatre were approved in May 1946, and the pouring of the concrete commenced in October 1946. The theatre opened on November 27, 1947. The architects, Kaplan and Sprachman, designed a modern yellow-brick structure with a soaring sign above the marquee that reached high into the air, B&F at its pinnacle.

B&F was a company created in 1927 by Jack M. Fine and Samuel Bloom. It grew throughout the years and eventually controlled twenty-one theatres. Samuel Bloom died in 1969 and his partner purchased his shares.

Ontario Archives, RG 56-11-0-324-4

Auditorium of the Vaughan Theatre.

Jack Fine sold B&F to Famous Players on June 22, 1970. The Vaughan was one the company's finest theatres.

I shall always remember visiting the Vaughan Theatre. After entering the lobby, the candy bar was ahead, down several steps, along the north wall. The auditorium was accessed by ascending two gently sloping ramps, located on the east and west sides of the lobby. The auditorium contained almost a thousand seats arranged in rows in the "stadium style." Designs on the walls and ceiling contained simple attractive lines that guided the eye toward the screen, the focal point of the interior space. Generous layers of drapery surrounded the screen, creating a luxurious feeling, especially when the curtains swept open at the beginning of a film.

I attended the Vaughan Theatre often until our family relocated to the west end of the city in 1953. The theatre closed in the 1980s and was demolished. Today, the site contains some undistinguished buildings that add nothing to the streetscape.

CHAPTER ELEVEN

Theatres on Eglinton Avenue West

AVENUE THEATRE

The Avenue Theatre at 331 Eglinton Avenue West, at the corner of Braemar Avenue, was one block west of Avenue Road. Built in the Art Deco style, its façade possessed a rounded corner on the west side, facing Eglinton Avenue. There were decorative designs under its cornice.

The auditorium contained 555 seats on the ground floor and 126 in the balcony. The Avenue's architectural plans were submitted to the city in June 1938. The licence was granted to the Waterloo Theatre Company Limited, and in 1938 Julio and Julius Edison were the managers. This is one of the old movie theatres about which I discovered very little information, other than it was demolished, likely in the 1960s, and shops were constructed on the site.

EGLINTON THEATRE

In my mind the Eglinton Theatre, along with the University Theatre, is forever associated with megahit films that played for many weeks and sometimes several years. Most of them were "hard-ticket reserved-seat" shows, requiring patrons to purchase tickets in advance of the date. In the industry, theatres that screened these types of films were referred

Toronto Archives, Fonds 1257, Series 1057, Item 3848

The Avenue Theatre in 1957.

City of Toronto Archives, Series 1278, File 68

Eglinton Theatre at 400 Eglinton Avenue West in 1947.

to as "Roadshow Houses." The Eglinton was one of them, and by agreement when such films were screened, no other theatre featured the same film unless it was located ninety miles or more from the Eglinton. This assured the theatre of exclusivity. Films screened between megahits were referred to as "fillers."

One of the best examples of a "hard-ticket" film at the Eglinton was *The Sound of Music*, screened from March 10, 1965, to December 21, 1967. Twentieth Century Fox Studios, the producers of the film, insisted on handling the opening night in Toronto. Though they did not own the theatre, they shipped new projectors from the United States, encased in bubble wrap. A new screen was installed to permit the film to be viewed in Todd-AO. Further improvements included new seating and carpeting. The studio also brought in their own staff for opening night, insisting that the Eglinton's regular staff step aside. Snacks, popcorn, and drinks were prepared in advance for the intermission. I remember seeing *The Sound of Music* at the Eglinton in 1965 and was greatly impressed with the theatre and film.

In the days after the opening of the film, daily performances were at 8:15 p.m., ending at 11:30 p.m., with Wednesday afternoon matinees at 2 p.m. The matinees were well-attended by seniors, who tended to avoid the evening shows as they ended at too late an hour. The matinees were also popular with school groups. One of the employees of the theatre caught the chicken pox due to being in contact with so many children.

Other long-running films that played at the Eglinton were *Windjammer: The Voyage of the Christian Radich* in Cinemascope in 1958, *How the West Was Won* (1962), *Dr. Doolittle* (1967), *Finian's Rainbow* in 1968, and *Hello, Dolly!* in 1969. To promote the film *Dr. Doolittle*, a press luncheon was held at the Queen Elizabeth Theatre at the CNE. In 1983 the James Bond movie *Octopussy* was shown, but it was not a hard-ticket screening.

For the opening of *Hello, Dolly!* a life-size photo of Barbra Streisand, attired in a white gown, was placed in a prominent position in the lobby. A Toronto graphic-design studio and the manager of the theatre created the picture from a cut-out. It depicted Streisand descending a red-carpeted staircase, as if she were in New York's Harmonia Gardens.

Unable to obtain palm trees, a local florist supplied tall corn stalks with fluffy tassels, which were placed in two large urns on either side of the picture. Fox Studios loved it.

The Eglinton Theatre has a distinguished record in the history of Toronto's movie theatres, beginning during the Great Depression of the 1930s. At the time, the district was in the early stages of development as a residential district. An immigrant from Sicily, Agostino Arrigo Senior, realized its potential and purchased property on the north side of Eglinton Avenue, a short distance west of Avenue Road, in the district of Forest Hill.

In this decade, securing financing for projects was extremely difficult. Agostino Arrigo dreamed of creating the finest theatre in the city, reasoning that, despite the Depression, movies would remain popular since they were inexpensive compared with other forms of entertainment. His faith was rewarded when he finally arranged financing with Famous Players Theatres. The Eglinton Theatre emerged from dream into reality.

The theatre's architects were Kaplan and Sprachman, who designed the theatre in the Art Deco style, with rounded corners and geometric shapes, accompanied by whimsical ornamental designs inspired by the Century of Progress International Exposition, the Chicago World's Fair of 1933. When the Eglinton opened, in 1936, it was hailed as being futuristic — Toronto's best modern theatre. It won the Governor General's Award for architectural excellence in 1937.

The theatre cost $200,000 to construct, an enormous amount of money during the Great Depression. The 800-seat auditorium was recessed from the street, parallel to Eglinton Avenue. Shops flanked the south side of the theatre that fronted on the sidewalk. The rent from these stores helped to offset the expenses of operating the theatre. The huge curved marquee covered the entire entrance area, the sign above it boldly displaying the name of the theatre. The sign was one of the tallest in the city, rivalling the great sign of the Imperial Theatre on Yonge Street.

City of Toronto Archives, Series 1278, File 68

Auditorium of the Eglinton in 1947.

When the Eglinton opened on April 2, 1936, the film that was screened was *King of Burlesque*. The decorative features of the interior amazed the audience. There were chandeliers, hand-carved statues, and glass-etched panels surrounded by attractive colours. The lobby even contained a fireplace.

Though theatre attendance declined in the decades ahead, the Eglinton remained profitable, as it was a premier venue. However, similar to most theatres, it struggled as the twenty-first century dawned. When the city demanded that wheelchair access be installed, its owners decided that the cost of this renovation was not practical, and it was finally shuttered in April 2002. Fortunately, it was not demolished, and it survives today as a special events venue, The Eglinton Grand.

Note: The author is grateful to Michael Allen Bronstorph for information on the Eglinton Theatre. Besides holding other positions in the theatre industry, he was the manager of the Eglinton for several years.

NORTOWN THEATRE

When I was in high school in the 1950s, I worked as a delivery boy for Crosstown Pharmacy, near the corner of Bathurst Street and Eglinton Avenue West. The owner of the store was Ed Greene, the brother of Lorne Greene, the actor who starred at the Stratford Theatre in its early years and later became famous for an American TV show called *Bonanza*, about a father and three sons who lived on a ranch named the Ponderosa.

A short distance west of the pharmacy was the Nortown Theatre, at 875 Eglinton Avenue West, on the south side of the street, between Bathurst and Peveril Street. After high school classes ended for the day, I travelled to work on my bicycle and regularly passed this theatre. Because the theatres in my own neighbourhood were older and less modern, I considered the Nortown luxurious and longed to attend it. When *The African Queen*, starring Katharine Hepburn and Humphrey Bogart, played at the theatre in 1951, I finally attended the theatre. Needless to say, I was duly impressed.

Ontario Archives, RG 56-11-0-303-6

Nortown Theatre in 1948, with the film Sitting Pretty *on the marquee. This was the first movie screened when the theatre opened.*

The Nortown opened on March 17, 1948. It was located in the south-east section of an area that in the early decades of the twentieth century was a rural district named Bedford Park-Nortown. In those years, it was forest and farmland to the north of the city. Bedford Park-Nortown extended from Eglinton Avenue north to today's Highway 401. Bathurst was its western boundary and Yonge Street its eastern. It is likely that the Nortown Theatre derived its name from this district, as did the Bedford Theatre on Yonge Street.

On the ground floor of the front of the Nortown Theatre there were extensive stainless-steel-framed windows that allowed the lobby to be visible from the street. The round box office was to the right of the entrance, which possessed large glass doors. The furniture in the lobby and foyer was contemporary, meant to appeal to the residents of the expensive homes in the area. Its auditorium contained almost a thousand seats, which were plush and well-padded to create a feeling of luxury. The floor of the theatre was maroon red, as dye had been added to the concrete

Ontario Archives, RG 56-11-0-303-4

Interior of the Nortown.

before it was poured, the colouring removing the necessity of painting the floor every three or four years. On the second floor of the Nortown there were offices.

The theatre screened several hard-ticket reserved-seat films. In 1966 *My Fair Lady* played at the theatre for seven weeks after departing the University. In 1966–67 *Doctor Zhivago* screened there for sixty-one weeks after leaving the University. *Paint Your Wagon* was another long-run film at the Nortown.

In the 1970s, as theatre attendance lessened, and because the price of land near Bathurst and Eglinton had greatly increased, the theatre was listed on the real estate market for $890,000. It eventually sold and was demolished in 1974. A small low-rise strip mall is now on the site.

CHAPTER TWELVE

Theatres on Other Streets
West of Yonge

ADELPHI THEATRE (CUM BAC)

I was unable to discover the year that the Adelphi Theatre opened, but it was likely in the 1920s. Its original name was the Cum Bac, likely a play on words, as the owners hoped that patrons would come back to the theatre as often as possible. The building was two storeys, with residential apartments on the second floor, located at 1008 Dovercourt Road, on the west side of the street, a short distance north of Bloor Street West. With only 460 plush seats, covered with leatherette, it was an intimate theatre. There was no balcony and only one aisle, in the centre of the auditorium, with six seats on either side.

In December 1933 a stink bomb exploded in the Cum Bac. The odour was so intense that one woman fainted. After the building was evacuated, it was discovered that a vagrant had committed the odoriferous deed. He was arrested, and when the case went to court, he was found guilty.

When the theatre was renovated in 1936 by the architectural firm of Kaplan and Sprachman, the name was changed to the Adelphi. In 1943 the theatre was again updated, the alterations designed by Jay English. I was unable to discover the year that the theatre closed, but it was likely about 1956. The asking price in that year was $60,000 for the entire building.

The Adelphi (Cum Bac) Theatre in 1936.

City of Toronto Archives, 1278, File 10

LANSDOWNE THEATRE (PARK, ACROPOLIS)

The Lansdowne Theatre was a neighbourhood movie house located at 683 Lansdowne Avenue, on the east side of the street a short distance north of Bloor Street. For many years, the old Lansdowne streetcars rumbled past the theatre. In the 1920s this streetcar line was well-known, because at the north end of its route, a short distance south of St. Clair Avenue, the line negotiated one of the steepest hills in Toronto. The gradation was so severe that the line required a sharp bend at the halfway point in order for streetcars to make it up. In early days, as a safety precaution, conductors employed handbrakes when descending the hill to prevent the streetcar from crashing down toward Davenport Road. The hill remains today, but there are no longer any Lansdowne streetcars, and the hill is far less threatening in an automobile.

The files in the Toronto Archives indicate that the Lansdowne Theatre opened in the late-1920s, although several websites suggest that it was in the mid-1930s. I admit that the theatre's architectural style resembles the

Toronto Archives, Ken Webster Collection, Series 1278, File 129

The Lansdowne Theatre on September 24, 1952.

Depression era more than that of the 1920s. The original name was the Park Theatre, but it was changed to the Lansdowne in 1937. Perhaps the name change explains the different dates given for the opening.

The theatre possessed a plain façade and an equally unornamented cornice, although there were brick patterns that rose vertically from above the canopy. There were apartments on the second floor. The auditorium had a concrete floor, with slightly over a thousand plush seats and no balcony. On the main floor there were two aisles.

In the theatre's interior there was little ornamentation. The walls and ceiling possessed straight lines and rectangular designs. The lobby was comfortably furnished and contained several large ashtrays. A refreshment bar was installed in 1948.

Sometime in the 1960s, the theatre's name was changed to the Acropolis and it screened Greek films. However, it eventually became less and less financially viable. The Lansdowne closed on July 13, 1961.

HILLCREST THEATRE

The Hillcrest is another of the old neighbourhood theatres that I never knew existed until I began researching the former movie houses of Toronto. The 1949 photo is the only one I was able to locate that depicts the theatre at 285 Christie Street, on the east side, a short distance south of Dupont Street — an area that was residential as well as industrial. The railway tracks that cross over Christie Street are visible in the picture. In the photo the theatre appears to have an attractive canopy and marquee, with a sign that was undoubtedly well-lit at night.

The original plans for the theatre were submitted to the city in 1922. The Hillcrest was a rectangular, two-storey brick building, with a concrete floor, 440 wooden seats, and two aisles. A notation in the Toronto Archives states that it is thought to have been designed by W.C. Hunt and J.L. Pennock. I have been unable to confirm this information or discover anything about these architects. When it opened, it possessed no marquee and its box office bordered the sidewalk.

City of Toronto Archives, Series 1278, File 82

This poor quality photo shows the Hillcrest Theatre in the distance in March 1949. The view looks north on Christie Street from south of Dupont Street. The theatre is on the right-hand side of the photo.

The Hillcrest was renovated in November 1930 and, strangely, again in January 1931, the latter renovations by Jay English, who relocated the box office, placing it inside the lobby on the right-hand side. Perhaps this was when the marquee and signage were added to the façade. The theatre was air-conditioned in 1937, and new seats were installed. The number of seats was reduced to 425, arranged in a pattern of six seats in the centre section and four on either side. On the second floor, above the projection booth, space was rented to a dentist.

On November 26, 1947, the theatre was robbed at gunpoint when Gilbert Roland (the Cisco Kid) was playing in the film *Beauty and the Bandit*. The cashier said that the thief, who stole just $27, was very polite. However, the thief's language might not have been so polite when he discovered the small amount of money in the cashier's drawer.

The theatre was refurbished in 1952, but like many neighbourhood theatres, it had difficulty competing with television. After the theatre closed, the building was converted for other purposes.

MAYFAIR THEATRE

The Mayfair Theatre at 347 Jane Street opened in September 1927. It was located on the east side of the street, a short distance south of Annette Street. When it opened, the surrounding community was a remote suburb northwest of the downtown area. The theatre mostly attracted people from the surrounding area, as there was no TTC service. The Mayfair was relatively modest in size, containing 478 seats, the centre section having eight seats, with five seats on either side. There was no balcony. The air-conditioning was filtered water-washed air.

In 1942 the Roseland Bus Line commenced service in the area. The bus route began at the Junction (Dundas and Keele Streets), travelled north on Keele to St. Clair, where Keele Street changed its name to Weston Road, then continued north to Lambton Avenue, where it turned west to Jane Street. The route then turned south to travel on Jane to Annette Street, where the route terminated. The Mayfair Theatre was located at the Roseland bus's southern terminus. This was

Mayfair Theatre in April 1959.

The Mayfair Theatre in 1928, the year after it opened. The view is south on Jane Street from near Annette Street. The houses on the opposite side of Jane Street (west side) remain in 2016. There is a vacant building lot on the north side of the theatre. Empty building lots are also visible further down the street, on the west side.

advantageous for the theatre, since it was easier for people to reach it by transit.

In the 1950s I attended Runnymede Collegiate on Jane Street, a ten-minute walk north of the Mayfair Theatre. Many of the students regularly attended the theatre.

The theatre closed in April 1959 and the building was listed on the real estate market at the price of $58,000. It was eventually purchased and converted for other retail purposes.

MOUNT DENNIS THEATRE (MAPLE LEAF)

The Mount Dennis Theatre opened in 1927 at 1006 Weston Road, on the west side of the street north of Eglinton Avenue. It was originally named the Maple Leaf Theatre, but was renamed the Mount Dennis in 1929. When the postal numbers were changed, its address became 1298 Weston Road.

When the theatre opened in 1929, Mount Dennis was a small town on the northwest fringe of the city. The old single-track trolley cars connected the town to the Junction area, situated at Keele and Dundas Street West. I remember travelling on these streetcars to the town of Weston when I was a boy in the 1940s. The privately owned theatre was built to serve the needs of the local residents. In the 1920s, the theatre's location was at the north end of Mount Dennis's business district, and in its heyday the theatre attracted many patrons.

I remember the theatre well, although I was never inside. In 1956 and 1957 I had an after-school job at the Reward Shoe Store in Weston. In those days, Jane Street ended at Lambton Avenue, as the road that today descends through Eglinton Flats had not been constructed. The rich alluvial soil of the Flats was then employed for market gardening.

Unfortunately, the Flats were severely flooded in 1954, when Hurricane Hazel devastated the city. Because of the floods, the area became part of the Metropolitan Conservation Authority, and no homes were permitted in the flood-prone area. During the next few years, the two sections of Jane Street were connected. Prior to this, when I bicycled from home to the town of Weston, I was forced to travel east along Lambton Avenue and

The Mount Dennis Theatre after it closed, when it was shabby and neglected.

then north on Weston Road to reach the shoe store. On these occasions, I passed the Mount Dennis Theatre. Today, the Eglinton Flats contain parkland and a public golf course.

In August 1959, the Mount Dennis Theatre was offered for sale at the asking price of $65,000, which included the apartments on the second floor. The real estate listing suggested that it would be ideal for a bowling alley or furniture store. However, when the theatre was purchased, it continued to operate as a movie house until 1975. After it closed, the building was employed for various commercial enterprises until eventually it was demolished. Today an apartment building stands on the site.

REVUE THEATRE

The Revue Theatre at 400 Roncesvalles Avenue is one of the oldest surviving movie houses in Toronto, its only rival for this distinction being the Fox Theatre on Queen Street East. Both theatres opened between 1912 and 1913 and remain active today. Their façades are unchanged from when they opened, although the original marquees on both theatres have been removed as they were too costly to maintain.

Because of the Revue's location, I was never inside it as a teenager. However, in 2013, during Doors Open Toronto, I journeyed on the streetcar to visit it. I had my choice of boarding either a King or a College streetcar, as the theatre is located near the intersection of Roncesvalles and Howard Park Avenues. This made me realize the advantage of the theatre's location in earlier decades, when almost everyone moved around the city by streetcar. On arrival I was impressed with the young volunteers who enthusiastically talked about the Revue and provided tours of the space behind the screen. They also allowed access to the projection room. Free popcorn was available at the candy bar — a generous touch.

In the mid-nineteenth century the area known as Parkdale, to the south of where the Revue is located today, was relatively undeveloped. However, it was expanding rapidly, even though it was considered remote from downtown. Because of its highly desirable location beside the lake, Parkdale

Ontario Archives, RG 56-11-0-314-1

The Revue Theatre in 1938.

attracted more and more permanent residents. Large Victorian-style homes increasingly appeared on its tree-lined streets. As a result, it was annexed to the City of Toronto in 1889. As land prices increased further and vacant residential lots disappeared, development relocated northward, along Roncesvalles Avenue. This street derived its name from a mountain pass in the Pyrenees where a battle was fought in the Napoleonic Wars.

As the area of Roncesvalles near Howard Park Avenue became more populated, it was obvious that building a movie theatre in the area could be a profitable enterprise. Thus, between the years 1912 and 1913, the Revue Theatre was constructed. Though in a quiet neighbourhood to the northwest of the downtown core, it benefitted from being close to two streetcar lines and surrounded by residential streets with ever-increasing populations to the east and west of Roncesvalles.

The Revue is not a large theatre, containing only around 500 seats. However, its size is appropriate for a local theatre that depended mainly on the surrounding community for patrons, supplemented by those who arrived by streetcar. The theatre's Fabricord seats were comfortable, and its two aisles provided easy entrances and exits from the theatre. This was an advantage in an era when moviegoers entered and departed constantly, rather than arriving at the starting time of a film. Despite the theatre's modest size, it possessed an impressive marquee. The façade displayed classical designs, with Greek dentils and Doric columns. The cornice on the peaked roof and the horizontal lower cornice below it also contained classical decorative detailing. The interior possessed designs with geometric shapes and patterns.

In the 1980s, the theatre became part of the Festival Theatre chain. However, in 2006 the company closed the Revue. It appeared as if a developer might purchase the property and demolish it. Fortunately, concerned residents raised funds to ensure its survival as a functioning movie house. The Revue reopened the following year, operated by the non-profit Revue Film Society.

In February of the year it reopened, a section of the marquee collapsed to the sidewalk, likely caused by the weight of the snow. For safety reasons, it was necessary to remove the entire marquee. A part of it was preserved by storing it in an area behind the screen.

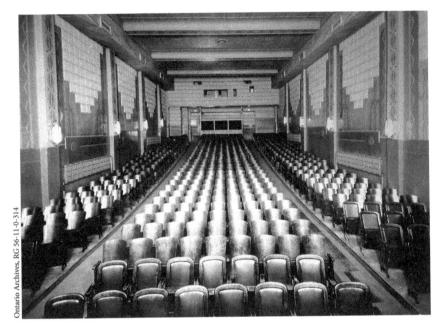

Ontario Archives, RG 56-11-0-314

Revue Theatre's auditorium.

Thankfully, the Revue Cinema remains open today and continues to offer nightly screenings. It is one of Toronto's remaining neighbourhood theatres of yesteryear.

BRIGHTON THEATRE

When the Brighton opened, it was an intimate theatre with approximately 400 wooden seats, the backs of the seats covered with leatherette. Located at 127 Roncesvalles, on the northeast corner of Galley and Roncesvalles Avenues, the Brighton was an integral part of the community for many decades.

The theatre was the equivalent of three floors in height, with three apartments on the top floor. The auditorium of the theatre occupied two storeys, with a floor that sloped toward the screen. There was no balcony. The red-brick structure possessed a rather unadorned cornice on its west façade, facing Roncesvalles, the exception being a row of

One of the few surviving photos of the Brighton Theatre.

large modillions (bracket-like ornamentations) below the cornice. In the decades ahead, the ground-floor level of the front of the theatre displayed canary-yellow tiles, creating a colourful sight for those passing on the street.

On its south façade, on Galley Avenue, there was even less detail, with straight, simple lines. The apartments above the theatre enjoyed much sunlight in winter, as they contained windows that faced south.

The ticket office was to the right of the lobby. There was no air-conditioning, but there were fans on either side of the screen that circulated the air. The Brighton was originally licensed to Clarence and William Welsman. A file in the Toronto Archives states that for many years, prior to the beginning of the evening's first film, a recording of "God Save the King" was played. Many theatres preformed this ritual in earlier decades, although some of them played the anthem at the end of the final movie of the evening.

I was unable to discover when the Brighton closed, but a letter in the Toronto Archives dated September 25, 1978, confirms that it was operating in that year. After the theatre closed, the ground-floor premises were remodelled to create retail space. In 2016 a grocery store occupied the first-floor level of the building where the old Brighton Theatre once welcomed its patrons for a night's movie entertainment.

GRANT THEATRE

I chose the Grant as the final theatre to be explored in this book because, of all the theatres mentioned in these pages, my fondest memories are attached to this theatre. It was where I attended my first Saturday-afternoon matinee and where I met all the great film stars of my youth.

The Grant opened in 1930 as an independent theatre, owned by the Grant family. Located at 524 Oakwood Avenue, near the intersection of Vaughan Road and Oakwood Avenue, it was an advantageous site for a theatre, as the Oakwood streetcars and the Vaughan buses passed near its doors. Surrounding it were shops that created the atmosphere of a mini-village. The Oakwood Hotel, a short distance to the south, was the other entertainment attraction in the immediate area.

City of Toronto Archives, Series 1278, File 10

The Grant Theatre c. 1940.

When I first visited it in the 1940s, the theatre was already showing its age. However, as a child I didn't notice. For me, it was the most wonderful movie theatre in the entire world — a place of pure magic.

Memories of my first matinee at the Grant remain with me today. The first film that afternoon was a murder mystery that almost scared me to death. I recall gazing at my older brother, who appeared entranced with the plot and not frightened in the least. I sat glued to my seat, tighter than the chewing gum stuck to its underside. Somehow, I managed to survive.

The second feature starred Sonja Henie, the three-time Olympic champion who had become a movie star. I must admit that her graceful antics on the ice bored me. However, in the weeks ahead I saw enough exciting films to erase the memories of Sonja Henie. I was introduced to pirates, cowboys, detectives, assorted villains, comedians, and musical/dancing stars.

Favourite comedy teams that I saw at the Grant were Laurel and Hardy and Abbott and Costello. Their antics were enormously funny, much of their humour centring on the predicaments they encountered in daily life. Their style of comedy was familiar to me through radio programs, such as *The Life of Riley*, starring William Bendix, and *Amos and Andy*.

On Halloween 1949, my older brother decided he was too mature to go "shelling out," as we referred to it. The term "trick-or-treat" was unknown to us until we heard it on American TV shows. My brother attended the Grant Theatre to view free movies for Halloween, the event sponsored by the local business community. They reasoned that teenagers watching movies was preferable to their roaming the streets playing pranks. However, the evening ended early when kids began pelting the screen with apples, creating large holes in it. The Grant closed early and no more free Halloween movies were ever offered.

Even after we purchased our first black-and-white television in 1953, the Grant retained its attraction due to the big-screen format and the superior quality of the pictures compared with TV. However, as TV images improved, and with the introduction of colour TV, the Grant Theatre finally lost to our in-house entertainment.

Another event that helped destroy the appeal of movie theatres was the introduction of *Hockey Night in Canada*, during the 1952–53 season. The broadcasts commenced at 9 p.m., an hour after the puck dropped. This meant that the game was often into the second period before it appeared on our television sets. People sometimes joked that they hoped a fight had delayed the proceedings so they would be able to see more of the game.

With the commencement of the CBC broadcast, more people began staying home to watch the games. The first tavern/bar in Canada to broadcast hockey was the Horseshoe Tavern on Queen West near Spadina Avenue. Saturday nights "on the town" were no longer monopolized by the movie theatres. Toronto's entertainment scene was changing and movie houses were the losers.

In 1953 our family moved away from the area where the Grant was located. The theatre closed its doors in 1956. It was demolished, except for the exterior walls, and renovated for other commercial purposes.

When Toronto's local movie theatres of yesteryear dominated the entertainment scene, they brought to life exciting places and provided adventures beyond our wildest dreams. To some degree, films continue to fulfill this role, but not to the extent they did in former decades, due to the current dominance of social media and electronic devices.

For many people, recalling the movie theatres of former decades generates fond memories. Few pastimes are as pleasant as indulging in nostalgia, as it recalls days when we were younger. The past is familiar and comforting, unlike the future, which is unknown.

When Toronto's wonderful old theatres started shutting their doors, attendance had dwindled to the point where they were no longer profitable. Most of them were also located on prime real estate, which created considerable pressure to redevelop their sites for other purposes.

In my youth, I lived in the Fairbank District of Toronto, in the Township of York. This area later became the City of York and in 1998 was amalgamated with the City of Toronto. The Grant Theatre closed in 1956 and the Colony in 1958. When these theatres were active, the names of the films on the theatre marquees were well-known. In the months prior to the coronation of Elizabeth II in 1953, television sales soared, and they accelerated during the next few years. It was not long before the evening's TV programming became more important than the films playing at the local theatres.

CONCLUSION

As the 1950s progressed, automobile sales increased. Neighbourhoods inside the city lost their stability as families became more mobile. When I was a boy, on the streets surrounding our home families had lived in the same houses for many years, sometimes for two generations. In the early 1950s there was an exodus to the suburbs, fulfilling the dream of a new home in a modern subdivision on a larger building lot. The white picket fence and garage were not obligatory, but were also part of the dream. These communities were created for people who owned cars. The local theatres in the older neighbourhoods of the city lost to the suburbs as people drove to theatres with parking lots.

The old movie houses that remain from decades past are now repertory theatres, serving the cinematic needs of their local communities, or are venues for live theatre. The theatres of my youth have been replaced by multiplex theatres located in suburban plazas or large retail buildings in the downtown area.

Despite the disappearance of the local movie theatres, I am grateful that multiplexes, where I am able to view films in the large-screen format, still exist. I fear that this experience may too disappear. There are predictions that in the future most films will be released directly to electronic devices and only blockbuster films will be shown in theatres. I hope this never occurs, but the demands of the future will be determined by movie viewers.

Despite this somewhat gloomy prediction, there remains hope for the future of the few old theatres that remain. Toronto is maturing as a city and is now striving to preserve more of its architectural history. This includes former movie houses. Though the laws to accomplish this aim remain weak, the era of demolishing old buildings without considering their merit as heritage sites is drawing to a close. Developers are discovering that including heritage structures within their projects is highly profitable. Though almost all of the old theatres have been demolished, the few that remain, particularly those that are smaller, present possibilities for cultural centres, community theatres, or multipurpose venues. The redevelopment of the Paradise Theatre on Bloor Street is an excellent example of this concept.

Most of the larger theatres of old have also been demolished, their immense size having made them financially unviable. The University,

Loew's Uptown, Tivoli, and Shea's Hippodrome are prime examples. The city is fortunate that the Ontario government prevented Loew's Downtown (the Elgin and Winter Garden) from being demolished and that theatrical impresario Garth Drabinsky restored the Imperial (Pantages, Ed Mirvish Theatre) to its former glory. Today, every time I attend the latter venue, during the intermission I always walk down the aisle to the stage area and gaze up in wonder at the magnificent domed ceiling. It is visible proof of the importance that was placed on theatres in the past.

There is another theatre of considerable size from yesteryear that miraculously has survived into the modern era, but few realize it still exists, and its future is uncertain. At Spadina Avenue and Dundas Street, the Standard began its life in 1922 as a Yiddish playhouse, the first in Toronto. In 1934 the theatre was converted to show films and renamed the Strand. Finally, as theatre attendance declined, it became an infamous burlesque house called the Victory, which finally closed in 1975, giving way to a Chinese-language theatre that lasted until 1994. The theatre's ornate auditorium has sat unused ever since. It remains intact, though it is rarely opened, similar to the Winter Garden (above the Elgin), which was mothballed for many decades before it was rediscovered and restored.

The only time I have heard of the Victory being used during the last few years was as a distribution point for donated toys and gifts during the Christmas season. I remain hopeful that an entrepreneur will eventually realize the theatre's potential and rescue it. Though such a project appears daunting, when Spadina Avenue is redeveloped, if the plans include the former burlesque house, Toronto will truly have matured into a city that respects its old theatres. This would be a positive sign for heritage preservation in general.

I feel fortunate to have experienced Toronto's theatre scene from the days when movie houses were the kings of entertainment to the modern era.

If this book helps preserve a few memories and images of the local movie theatres of yesteryear, then my time will have been worthwhile.

INDEX

Numbers in italics indicate images

INDEX

INDEX

INDEX

DUNDURN

VISIT US AT

Dundurn.com
@dundurnpress
Facebook.com/dundurnpress
Pinterest.com/dundurnpress